Connecticut

THE THIRTEEN COLONIES

Connecticut

CRAIG A. DOHERTY

KATHERINE M. DOHERTY

Facts On File, Inc.

Connecticut

Facts On File, Inc.
132 West 31st Street
New York NY 10001

Library of Congress Cataloging-in-Publication Data
Doherty, Craig A.
   Connecticut / Craig A. Doherty and Katherine M. Doherty.
     p. cm. — (The thirteen colonies)
   Includes bibliographical references and index.
   ISBN 0-8160-5417-7
   1. Connecticut—History—Colonial period, ca. 1600–1775—Juvenile literature. 2. Connecticut —History—1775–1865—Juvenile literature. I. Doherty, Katherine M. II. Title.

   F94/3/D64 2006
   974.6'02—dc22   2004027533

Facts On File books are available at special discounts when purchased in bulk quantities for businesses, associations, institutions, or sales promotions. Please call our Special Sales Department in New York at (212) 967-8800 or (800) 322-8755.

You can find Facts On File on the World Wide Web at http://www.factsonfile.com

Text design by Erika K. Arroyo
Cover design by Semadar Megged
Maps and graph by Dale Williams

Printed in the United States of America

VB FOF 10 9 8 7 6 5 4 3 2 1

This book is printed on acid-free paper.

This book is dedicated to
the many students of all ages
we have worked with and taught over the years.

Note on Photos

Many of the illustrations and photographs used in this book are old, historical images. The quality of the prints is not always up to current standards, as in some cases the originals are from old or poor-quality negatives or are damaged. The content of the illustrations, however, made their inclusion important despite problems in reproduction.

Contents

Introduction

In the 11th century, Vikings from Scandinavia sailed to North America. They explored the Atlantic coast and set up a few small settlements. In Newfoundland and Nova Scotia, Canada, archaeologists have found traces of these settlements. No one knows for sure why they did not establish permanent colonies. It may have been that it was too far away from their homeland. At about the same time, many Scandinavians were involved with raiding and establishing settlements along the coasts of what are now Great Britain and France. This may have offered greater rewards than traveling all the way to North America.

When the western part of the Roman Empire fell in 476, Europe lapsed into a period of almost 1,000 years of war, plague, and hardship. This period of European history is often referred to as the Dark Ages or Middle Ages. Communication between the different parts of Europe was almost nonexistent. If other Europeans knew about the Vikings' explorations westward, they left no record of it. Between the time of Viking exploration and Christopher Columbus's 1492 journey, Europe underwent many changes.

By the 15th century, Europe had experienced many advances. Trade within the area and with the Far East had created prosperity for the governments and many wealthy people. The Catholic Church had become a rich and powerful institution. Although wars would be fought and governments would come and go, the countries of Western Europe had become fairly strong. During this time, Europe rediscovered many of the arts and sciences that had

Vikings explored the Atlantic coast of North America in ships similar to this one. *(National Archives of Canada)*

existed before the fall of Rome. They also learned much from their trade with the Near and Far East. Historians refer to this time as the Renaissance, which means "rebirth."

At this time, some members of the Catholic Church did not like the direction the church was going. People such as Martin Luther and John Calvin spoke out against the church. They soon gained a number of followers who decided that they would protest and form their own churches. The members of these new churches were called Protestants. The movement to establish these new churches is called the Protestant Reformation. It would have a big impact on America as many Protestant groups would leave Europe so they could worship the way they wanted to.

In addition to religious dissent, problems arose with the overland trade routes to the Far East. The Ottoman Turks took control of the lands in the Middle East and disrupted trade. It was at this time that European explorers began trying to find a water route to the Far East. The explorers first sailed around Africa. Then an Italian named Christopher Columbus convinced the king and queen of Spain that it would be shorter to sail west to Asia rather than go around Africa. Most sailors and educated people at the time knew the world was round. However, Columbus made two errors in his calculations. First, he did not realize just how big the Earth is, and second, he did not know that the continents of North and South America blocked a westward route to Asia.

When Columbus made landfall in 1492, he believed that he was in the Indies, as the Far East was called at the time. For a period of time after Columbus, the Spanish controlled the seas and the exploration of what was called the New World. England tried to compete with the Spanish on the high seas, but their ships were no match for the floating fortresses of the Spanish Armada. These heavy ships, known as galleons, ruled the Atlantic.

In 1588, that all changed. A fleet of English ships fought a series of battles in which their smaller but faster and more maneuverable ships finally defeated the Spanish Armada. This opened up the New World to anyone willing to cross the ocean. Portugal, Holland, France, and England all funded voyages of exploration to the New World. In North America, the French explored the far north. The Spanish had already established colonies in what are now Florida, most of the Caribbean, and much of Central and South America. The Dutch

Depicted in this painting, Christopher Columbus completed three additional voyages to the Americas after his initial trip in search of a westward route to Asia in 1492. *(Library of Congress, Prints and Photographs Division [LC-USZ62-103980])*

bought Manhattan and would establish what would become New York, as well as various islands in the Caribbean and lands in South America. The English claimed most of the east coast of North America and set about creating colonies in a variety of ways.

Companies were formed in England and given royal charters to set up colonies. Some of the companies sent out military and trade expeditions to find gold and other riches. They employed men such as John Smith, Bartholomew Gosnold, and others to explore the lands they had been granted. Other companies found groups of Protestants who wanted to leave England and worked out deals that let them establish colonies. No matter what circumstances a colony was established under, the first settlers suffered hardships as

After Columbus's exploration of the Americas, the Spanish controlled the seas, largely because of their galleons, or large, heavy ships, that looked much like this model. *(Library of Congress, Prints and Photographs Division, [LC-USZ62-103297])*

they tried to build communities in what to them was a wilderness. They also had to deal with the people who were already there.

Native Americans lived in every corner of the Americas. There were vast and complex civilizations in Central and South America. The city that is now known as Cahokia was located along the Mississippi River in what is today Illinois and may have had as many as 50,000 residents. The people of Cahokia built huge earthen mounds that can still be seen today. There has been a lot of speculation as to the total population of Native Americans in 1492. Some have put the number as high as 40 million people.

Most of the early explorers encountered Native Americans. They often wrote descriptions of them for the people of Europe. They also kidnapped a few of these people, took them back to Europe, and put them on display. Despite the number of Native Americans, the Europeans still claimed the land as their own. The rulers of Europe and the Catholic Church at the time felt they had a right to take any lands they wanted from people who did not share their level of technology and who were not Christians.

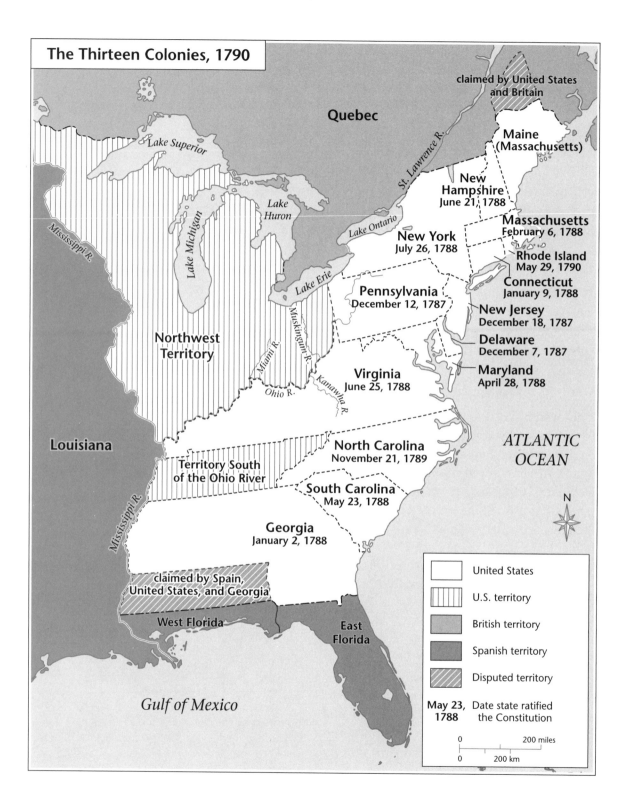

The Thirteen Colonies, 1790

Quebec

Lake Superior

Lake Michigan

Lake Huron

Lake Ontario

Lake Erie

St. Lawrence R.

Mississippi R.

claimed by United States
and Britain

Maine
(Massachusetts)

New
Hampshire
June 21, 1788

Massachusetts
February 6, 1788

Rhode Island
May 29, 1790

New York
July 26, 1788

Connecticut
January 9, 1788

Pennsylvania
December 12, 1787

New Jersey
December 18, 1787

Delaware
December 7, 1787

Maryland
April 28, 1788

Northwest
Territory

Miami R.

Muskingum R.

Ohio R.

Kanawha R.

Virginia
June 25, 1788

Louisiana

North Carolina
November 21, 1789

ATLANTIC
OCEAN

Territory South
of the Ohio River

South Carolina
May 23, 1788

Mississippi R.

Georgia
January 2, 1788

N

claimed by Spain,
United States, and Georgia

West Florida

East
Florida

Gulf of Mexico

	United States
	U.S. territory
	British territory
	Spanish territory
	Disputed territory

May 23, 1788   Date state ratified the Constitution

0   200 miles
0   200 km

First Contacts

EUROPEAN CLAIMS

In the 15th, 16th, and early 17th centuries, a number of explorers sailing for a variety of European governments visited the coast of North America. In 1497 John Cabot, an Italian employed by the English tried to find a new route to Asia by way of the Americas. Based on his voyage, England claimed much of North America even though it would be well over 100 years before there was a successful English colony on the continent. The French, Spanish, Swedes, and Dutch all made claims and established colonies in North America. The French claim was based on the 1525 voyage of Giovanni da Verrazano, who explored the coast from present-day North Carolina to Nova Scotia. The Dutch claimed all the land between the Delaware and Connecticut Rivers based on the voyage of Henry Hudson in 1609. In the ship the *Half Moon*, Hudson and his crew sailed up the river that now bears his name as far as present-day Albany, New York, and explored other rivers in the hope of finding a passage to Asia.

Sponsored by the Dutch East India Company, Henry Hudson explored in 1609 what would become known as the Hudson River in present-day New York. *(National Archives of Canada)*

After the ship Adriaen Block and his crew had sailed on to North America caught fire and sank, they built the *Onrust* and explored the present-day Connecticut coast. *(North Wind Picture Archives)*

Although Hudson never found a northern passage to Asia during any of his four voyages, he gave the Dutch a claim to the area they called New Netherland. At first, there were no permanent European settlements in New Netherland. Instead, ships loaded with trade goods sailed to the area and traded for furs with the American Indians who lived along the Hudson and Delaware Rivers. In 1613, Captain Adriaen Block arrived at Manhattan Island to trade for furs. While anchored near Manhattan, his ship the *Tiger* caught fire and sank. Block and his crew had to swim to shore. They were forced to spend the winter on the island and were able to survive because of the generosity of the local Indians.

In spring 1614, Block and his crew built a boat and sailed north in the hope of finding a ship big enough to take them back to the Netherlands. They cut down trees and used the timber to build the boat they called the *Onrust*, which means "restless." Aboard the *Onrust*, they sailed up the coast of what is now Connecticut. As Block and his men explored the coastline, they found a large river up which they could sail. The Indians of the area called the river the Quinnehtukqut, which means "long river." Over time, Europeans adopted this name for the river and the colony

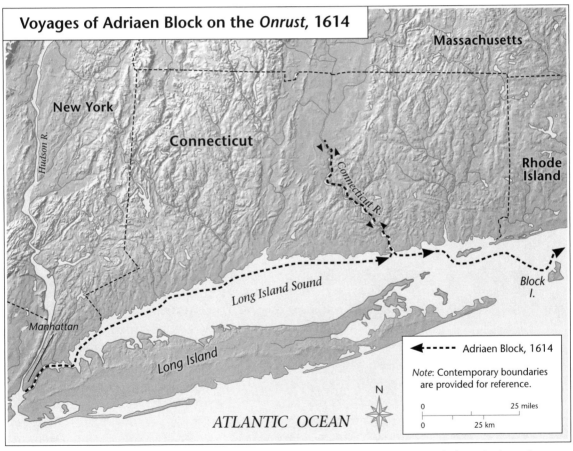

Voyages of Adriaen Block on the *Onrust*, 1614

Massachusetts

New York

Connecticut

Rhode Island

Hudson R.

Connecticut R.

Block I.

Long Island Sound

Manhattan

Long Island

◄----- Adriaen Block, 1614

Note: Contemporary boundaries are provided for reference.

0   25 miles
0   25 km

N

ATLANTIC OCEAN

Block and his crew built the *Onrust* in Manhattan after their ship sank. They then sailed north along the Connecticut coast before being picked up by a ship that took them to Europe.

that was founded on its banks, but they changed the spelling to Connecticut.

Block sailed upriver to the Indian village of Saukiog, which was located near present-day Hartford, Connecticut. Block and his crew spent two weeks with the people of Saukiog and traded for furs while they were there. They were probably the first Europeans to have contact with the American Indians who lived along the Connecticut River. Block then continued upriver into what is now northern Connecticut before he turned around and returned to Long Island Sound. He then sailed north and found an island off the coast of what is now Rhode Island. That island still bears the name of the adventurous Dutchman. Based on Block's exploration, the Dutch claimed the area surrounding the Connecticut River, but in the early years of the 17th century it did not matter what a country claimed. Instead, land went to those who created and maintained permanent settlements.

Despite a Dutch trading post on the Connecticut River, it was English Puritans from the Plymouth Colony and Massachusetts Bay Colony who eventually established Connecticut as one of the 13 original British colonies. However, they were by no means the first people to live in Connecticut. Numerous tribes of Algonquian-speaking American Indians had lived along the rivers and bays of Connecticut for thousands of years.

THE FIRST PEOPLE OF CONNECTICUT

When Adriaen Block and his crew sailed up the Connecticut River in 1614, there were probably more than 30,000 American Indians in what is now Connecticut. There were a number of tribes that varied in size from thousands of members to less than 100. The largest tribes were the Pequot, Niantic, Narragansett, and Nipmuck. The Narragansett territory was primarily in what is now Rhode Island, while the Nipmuck territory extended north into present-day Massachusetts. The smaller tribes included the Tunxis, Naugatuck, Quirpi, Wepawaug, Potatuck, Wangunk, and Podunk. The Podunk may have been the smallest tribe, with approximately 50 members living in one village of the same name. The word *podunk* is now used to describe any small and isolated community.

American Indians are classified by researchers in a number of ways. First is usually by the language they speak or spoke. Scien-

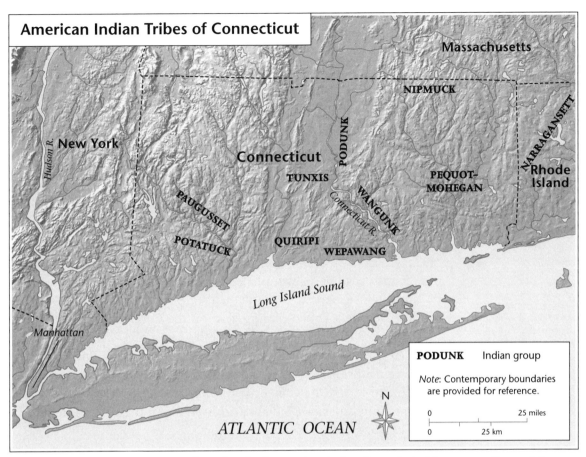

American Indian Tribes of Connecticut

Massachusetts

NIPMUCK

New York

Connecticut

PODUNK

TUNXIS

PEQUOT-
MOHEGAN

Rhode
Island

Hudson R.

PAUGUSSET

WANGUNK

Connecticut R.

POTATUCK

QUIRIPI

WEPAWANG

NARRAGANSETT

Long Island Sound

Manhattan

PODUNK   Indian group

Note: Contemporary boundaries
are provided for reference.

0   25 miles

0   25 km

N

ATLANTIC OCEAN

There were numerous American Indian tribes in Connecticut before the arrival of Europeans. Some of the larger ones are shown on this map.

tists have classified approximately 150 different language groups in North America. All the tribes in the area that is now Connecticut spoke a language that was part of the Algonquian language family. Scientists also classify tribes by the way they lived, which is referred to as their cultural group or culture area. In this respect, the Indians of Connecticut were also similar because they belonged to what is called the Eastern Woodland Culture or the Northeast culture area.

By the 17th century, Woodland Indians had a rich and varied culture that was dependent on the forest around them to fill many of their material needs. They were also accomplished farmers who grew corn, beans, and a variety of squashes for food. They grew

Corn

Corn was first domesticated 6,000 to 8,000 years ago in Central America. Its cultivation spread until it was grown throughout the temperate regions of North America. Corn is a member of the grass family. Through careful seed selection and hybridization, Native Americans were able to develop many varieties of corn and adapt its growth to a wide range of climatic zones. In Connecticut, the Native Americans grew three main varieties of corn. The most important type could be dried and ground into cornmeal to make a variety of dishes. They also grew a type of corn that was dried whole and added to soups and stews throughout the winter. It was also eaten fresh, like modern corn on the cob. They also cultivated a type of corn that was used as popcorn.

tobacco, which was smoked in pipes during a variety of religious ceremonies. Although corn was the most important part of their diet, they also ate a variety of nuts, berries, and other wild plants. In addition, the Indians of the area were accomplished hunters and fishers.

The rivers, lakes, and bays of the area were rich with a wide variety of fish and shellfish. The Indians of Connecticut used a number of fishing methods, including nets, spears, hooks and lines, and various types of fish traps. Lobsters, crabs, clams, oysters and other shellfish were easily gathered along the shore. In spring, the streams and rivers of Connecticut teemed with fish that traveled upriver to spawn. Where it was feasible, the Indians erected fish weirs to trap fish on spawning runs. A weir is a barricade, usually constructed of rocks, which forces fish to swim through a narrow channel where they can easily be speared, trapped, or netted.

The Indians of Connecticut were excellent hunters of both large and small game. They used their bows and arrows to take game. They also made traps to catch small animals and birds. Most important to Woodland Indians was the white-tailed deer. All parts of the deer were used. The meat was eaten alone fresh or dried and also dried to be added to stews later. Deerskins were tanned and used as the primary material for clothing. In addition, the bones and antlers of the deer were made into a variety of tools. Even the deer's hooves had a use. They were made into a variety of rattles that were used during the singing and dancing that were part of the numerous ceremonies that were an important aspect of Indian life.

Ceremonies marked numerous events during the year. One of the most important events was known as the Green Corn Festival. This festival was held in the early summer when the first of the year's corn crop was ready to be eaten fresh. This celebration marked the point in the year when the tribe knew its crops were going to succeed and that they would have food for the next winter. There were also celebrations to mark the time to collect various wild plants, berries, and nuts.

Religion was an integral part of everyday life for American Indians. They did not believe in one god as the Europeans did. Instead they believed that all parts of their world, both living and inanimate, were part of the spirit world. If they killed a deer, they would give thanks to the deer's spirit for their successful hunt. After a plentiful harvest, they would give thanks to the three sister spirits that represented corn, beans, and squash. In this way,

Native Americans used almost every part of the white-tailed deer that they killed. *(National Park Service)*

In this late 19th-century engraving published in *Harper's New Monthly Magazine,* Native Americans relax near their birch-bark wigwams, the type of homes many of the American Indians in present-day Connecticut inhabited. *(Library of Congress, Prints and Photographs Division [LC-USZ62-106105])*

they saw their lives as being in harmony with their world. In contrast, Europeans often saw nature as something to fight against and try to conquer. These different views of the world caused many misunderstandings between the two groups of people and ultimately led to the destruction of most of the American Indians of Connecticut.

All of the Indians of Connecticut lived in villages, and most of these villages were along the many rivers and streams of the area. The villages consisted of a number of structures where the people lived. Most of the tribes built round shelters known as wigwams. These were constructed by cutting a number of small, flexible trees

known as saplings. The thicker ends of the saplings were buried in a circle in the ground. The tops were bent into the middle to form a dome. The dome was then covered with woven mats or bark to keep the weather out. Low benches were built along the inside of the wigwam and could be used for sitting during the day and sleeping at night. A hole was left in the top for smoke from the winter cooking fires to escape. In the warmer months, people usually cooked outside.

The Pequot had only been in the area for around 100 years and had come from the area to the northwest that was controlled by the League of the Iroquois. Their connection to the powerful Iroquois tribes was evident in the shelters they built. The Pequot built what are referred to as longhouses. Instead of setting saplings in a circle, a longhouse was built by setting two parallel rows of saplings 15 to 30 feet apart. The saplings were then bent into the center to form a long, arch-shaped frame that might be 150 or more feet long. An additional frame was attached to strengthen the structure. Large sheets of bark were attached to the outside of the longhouse. The inside of a longhouse was divided into family apartments that were usually about 20 feet long. All the families in one longhouse were usually related.

Benches and shelves lined both sides of each apartment, and there was a walkway and space for winter cooking fires along the center of the structure. Slits were left in the roof for smoke to escape. Beds in both wigwams and longhouses were made of furs from a variety of animals. During the coldest times of the year, a

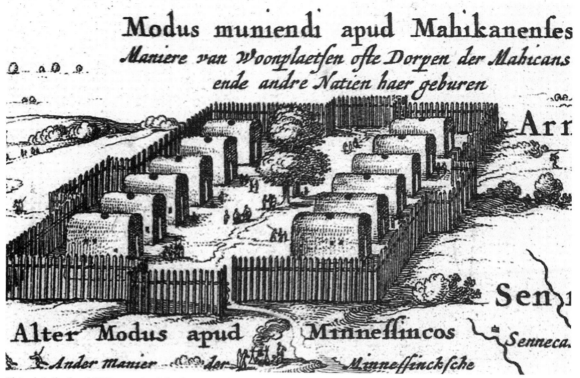

Modus muniendi apud Mahikanenſes
Maniere van Woonplaetſen ofte Dorpen der Mahicans
ende andre Natien haer geburen

Arr

Sen

Senneca.

Alter Modus apud Minneſſincos
Ander manier ... der Minneſſinckſche

This detail of a 1685 map by Nicolaes Visscher that was based on the explorations of Henry Hudson shows longhouses, which were divided into apartments and housed multiple American Indian families. *(Library of Congress)*

bearskin was a valuable blanket. Food and tools were stored on the shelves above the benches or hung from the ceiling. During the long winters, people gathered around the fires in their houses and told stories about their world and the people and spirits that inhabited it. Many of these stories were meant to teach the children and remind the adults about the history of the tribe and the proper way to live their lives.

The Indians had no written language and no formal schools. Children learned by listening to stories and helping the adults. Very early in life, children were expected to help in the fields and forests that yielded their families' subsistence. There was also a distinction between the work done by the women and that done by men. Women were primarily responsible for tending the fields while the men hunted and fished. However, for jobs that needed intense labor, everyone worked together. This included times when the fields needed tilling for spring planting or when fish were on the spring spawning runs.

Although there had been a certain amount of friction between the Pequot and the other tribes of the area, they mainly lived peacefully with each other. To protect themselves from attack, most of the villages had what is called a palisade constructed around it. A palisade was a wall of logs whose ends were buried in the ground and whose tops were sharpened to prevent enemies from climbing over. There was often trade among the tribes and clamshell beads known as wampum were an important trade good among the tribes.

When Europeans first began trading with the Indians of the area, they caused a number of changes among the Native peoples.

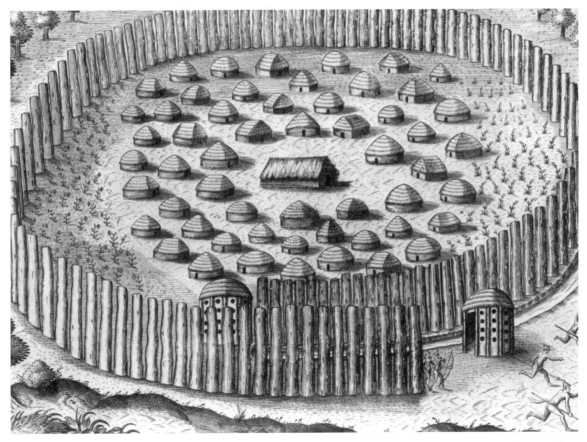

To protect themselves, some tribes built palisades (also called stockades), a perimeter around a village made of tall timbers, sharpened at one end and driven into the ground. *(Library of Congress)*

Wampum

The Indians of Connecticut, like many groups along the east coast of North America, made beads using clamshells. They used a variety of clamshells to create white beads, which were always more plentiful. They used the quahog clamshell to produce dark-colored beads that ranged in color from black to purple and blue. The beads were then strung on leather or hemp twine and fashioned into belts and jewelry.

Much of the wampum was used for decoration, but some wampum belts used a series of symbols to depict a story or send a message from one group to another. The Native Americans who had access to the coast often traded wampum for goods with other Indians in the interior of the continent.

The colonists soon began to use wampum as money. In the early years of the American colonies, there was little or no money available. At first, people exchanged food as a form of currency, but this had many drawbacks—the major one being its perishable nature. If not consumed quickly, the person accepting the food would soon lose his or her profit. To solve this problem, the colonists began to accept wampum in exchange for goods, and the colonial governments set exchange rates. Mass-produced English wampum created a number of trading problems among the Indians of the area because it reduced the value of Indian wampum that was made by hand.

In New Netherland, the exchange rate was set at four white beads equaling one stiver, which was the equivalent of an English pence. The black or dark-colored beads were worth twice as much. The last recorded use of wampum as money by European settlers took place in New York in 1701.

Wampum's uses ranged from recording agreements to sending messages, but its use as money became more important for tribes after the arrival of European explorers and settlers. *(National Archives, Still Picture Records, NWDNS-106-IN-18A)*

The introduction of metal tools and weapons, European cloth, and manufactured buttons and beads, caused many traditional practices and materials to be left behind. In addition, the competition for furs and trading rights brought a number of tribes into conflict with each other. The Pequot, who were the most numerous tribe in the area and had often fought in armed conflict, came to dominate trade with the Dutch. Disputes over trade first split the Pequot into two tribes: the Pequot and the Mohegan, and then led to the virtual destruction of the Pequot by the Europeans.

Many of the Indians of the area were killed or captured during wars. Those who were captured often ended up as slaves for other tribes or were sold to European plantations in the Caribbean Islands. Many other Indians in the area died from European diseases. Measles, mumps, and especially smallpox were usually fatal to American Indians. Epidemics of smallpox in the early years of the 17th century, introduced by fishermen along the coast of northern New England, wiped out many of the villages in what are now Maine and Massachusetts. Had the Indians of Connecticut known how they would suffer at the hands of European colonists they might have been less welcoming to Block and the early colonists who followed.

2

First Settlements in Connecticut

After the defeat of the Spanish Armada by England in 1588, Spanish control of the high seas ended. England, France, and the Netherlands all turned their attention to acquiring more colonies in North America and elsewhere. The French set their sights on the fur-rich lands along the Saint Lawrence River, where

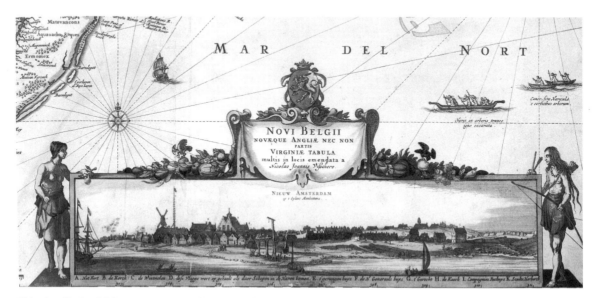

This detail of a 17th-century map of New Netherland by Nicolaes Visscher is a vignette of New Amsterdam, which would later become New York City. *(Library of Congress)*

Samuel de Champlain established the settlement of Quebec in 1608. For the Dutch, the voyage of Henry Hudson on his ship the *Half Moon* directed their attention to what is now called the Hudson River in New York. In 1624, they established a fort and trading post at what is now Albany, New York, and a settlement at what they called New Amsterdam. New Amsterdam's name would later be changed to New York City.

In the first years of the 17th century, two companies were formed in England to promote colonization in North America. The London Virginia Company was formed by businessmen in London and granted the right to start a colony in what is now Virginia. In 1607, the London Virginia Company sent a group of soldiers and adventurers to Chesapeake Bay where they established Jamestown. The other group, the Plymouth Virginia Company, was given the right to colonize land north of the London

John Winthrop was the first governor of Massachusetts Bay Colony. *(Library of Congress, Prints and Photographs Division [LC-USZ62-124240])*

Virginia Company's claim. Instead of organizing a military-style expedition as had been done in Virginia, the businessmen in Plymouth had a different plan.

They recruited a group of religious separatists to establish a colony on the lands the company had been granted by the king. In 1620, a group referred to as "Pilgrims" set sail on the *Mayflower* from Plymouth, England, for North America. When they arrived in what is now Massachusetts, they found a good spot for a community. The land had already been cleared by American Indians but had been abandoned when the local tribe was wiped out by smallpox. They named the colony they established there Plymouth. Plymouth Colony remained relatively small and later became part of Massachusetts.

Ten years later, a company known as the Massachusetts Bay Company was organized in London and included the Puritan leader John Winthrop. Along with other Puritan leaders, Winthrop hoped to establish a colony at Massachusetts Bay where Puritans

Pilgrims and Puritans

During the 16th century, a number of religious thinkers in Europe became unhappy with the practices of the Catholic Church. In protest, some of these people started new churches and were called Protestants. In England in 1532, King Henry VIII had a serious problem. He wanted to divorce his wife Catherine of Aragon and marry his pregnant lover Anne Boleyn. However, the Catholic Church did not allow divorce. To solve his personal problem and strengthen the English government, Henry VIII declared himself head of the English church and therefore independent from the pope in Rome.

He was quickly granted his divorce and married Anne Boleyn, but this move opened the door in England for Protestants who also had disagreements with the Catholic Church. For many, just breaking away from the Catholic Church was not enough. They wanted considerable changes in the church. Those who saw little hope of the Church of England changing enough to conform with their beliefs left the church and were known as Separatists. The government in England persecuted these people, putting some in prison and forcing others to flee to Holland and other places in Europe that were more tolerant of people's differing beliefs. The Pilgrims who settled Plymouth Colony were Separatists seeking a place where they could worship as they saw fit.

Many other people who wanted to reform the Church of England remained members of the church. It was their belief that they would eventually be able to purify the practices of the church from within. These people were known as Puritans, and they increasingly found themselves persecuted by church leaders and the government. It was from this group of Puritans that John Winthrop recruited colonists for the Massachusetts Bay Colony. It was their intent to create a religious colony that conformed to their Puritan views.

would be free to practice their religious beliefs without interference. In 1630, Winthrop led a large, well organized group of colonists to Massachusetts Bay, where they established Boston and a number of other towns.

As colonies grew in Plymouth, Massachusetts Bay, and New Netherland, the area that is now Connecticut remained inhabited by numerous tribes of American Indians. People from all three colonies looked to the lands along the Connecticut River as a place to expand their colonies. The Dutch had regularly taken trading trips up the Connecticut River since Captain Adriaen Block had first made contact in the area in 1614. They considered all the land between the Hudson and Connecticut Rivers part of New Netherland. In 1633, the Dutch wanted a more permanent presence in Connecticut and built a fort and trading post, which they named the House of Hope. It was located on the river at what is now Hartford, Connecticut.

A year earlier, just prior to the establishment of the Dutch fort, Edward Wilson had explored the area at the request of Governor William Bradford of the Plymouth Colony. Bradford hoped to establish trade with the Indians of the area and tried to get the leaders in Massachusetts Bay to join him. The leaders in Plymouth went ahead with their plans and built a trading post upriver from the Dutch in 1633. They called their new settlement Windsor.

In fall 1634, a group led by John Oldham of Watertown in the Massachusetts Bay Colony, started a settlement called Wethersfield, which was just south of the Dutch. All three settlements began

The Dutch built a trading post known as House of Hope at the location of present-day Hartford, Connecticut, in 1633. *(North Wind Picture Archives)*

with the idea of promoting the fur trade with the Indians who lived in the area. The Dutch had established trading relations with the Pequot, the most powerful tribe in the area. The Pequot monopolized the trade, forcing less powerful tribes to trade through them. It was in part because of this arrangement that many of the tribes along the river welcomed the arrival of the English traders so they could trade with them directly without going through the Pequot middlemen.

Although the initial interest in the land along the Connecticut River was for purposes of trade, that soon changed. The Plymouth and Massachusetts Bay Colonies were both created so that people could practice their religion without interference from the government and church in England. However, it is wrong to believe that these people were interested in religious tolerance. Both the Puritans and Pilgrims expected people to live according to the strict laws of the church. In addition, since the leaders of the churches and the colonies were often the same people, there was little difference between the laws of the church and the laws of the government. In fact, only male members of the church were allowed to vote, and the churches made it hard to become a member.

In this climate of strict church rule, those who had any disagreement with the church were often severely punished. In the first 10 years after the establishment of Massachusetts Bay Colony, members who disagreed with the church often left and formed other colonies in what would become New Hampshire, Rhode Island, and Connecticut. In addition to disagreements over religious doctrine, the best land in Plymouth and Massachusetts Bay colony was quickly taken up.

The colonists who arrived in New England quickly claimed the natural meadows and marshes that lined the area's bays and rivers for use as farmland. This land readily provided areas where farms could be established with very little extra effort. The grasses that grew in the marshes made excellent hay for livestock and the natural meadows along the rivers were easily plowed. Colonists who were forced to clear the forest to create farmland faced a more difficult task.

Their only tools were broadaxes, picks, shovels, and oxen. Away from the river valleys, even after the trees had been cut

In 1636, Reverend Thomas Hooker led about 100 of his parishioners from Massachusetts Bay Colony to Hartford, a town some of Hooker's followers had founded next to the Dutch fort House of Hope the previous year. In this cartoon drawn in the 1890s, Hooker stands next to a sick woman on a stretcher and gestures toward the valley they are about to enter. *(Library of Congress, Prints and Photographs Division [DRWG/US—Niehaus, no. 1])*

down, the settlers had to remove a seemingly endless supply of rocks from the soil. The thousands of miles of stone walls that line the New England countryside to this day stand as a testament to the untold effort it took to make the land suitable for farming. When word reached Massachusetts Bay Colony that the rich, low-lying lands of the Connecticut River valley awaited anyone willing to move, many people became even more interested in Connecticut.

Reverend Thomas Hooker was one of many religious leaders in Massachusetts who did not see eye-to-eye with the leaders of the

Life on the Frontier

It may be difficult for some to think of Hartford, Connecticut, as a frontier, but in 1635 that is exactly what it was. Those who arrived at Hartford in 1635 had to face an unusually cold winter with little time to prepare. Many people were forced to live in "dugouts" in the sides of the area's hills. A dugout was created by digging a hole in the hillside and then lining it with logs or stones. A roof was made of poles that were covered with bark and mud plaster. As supplies dwindled that first winter in Hartford, the English settlers were saved by the generosity of the local Indians who gave them enough food to survive. Some settlers were forced to return to Massachusetts for part of the winter but returned in the spring with Hooker.

After that first winter, most of the dugouts were replaced with wooden houses. The typical house on the frontier was relatively small, consisting of one or two rooms. Most of these houses had a large fireplace at one end of the building that was used for both heat and cooking. As time went on, many of the settlers added on to their houses or built bigger houses.

colony. He and the members of his church in Newtown (Cambridge), across the river from Boston, decided they would be better off if they left Massachusetts. In 1635, some of Hooker's followers moved to the Connecticut River valley and started the town of Hartford next to the Dutch fort.

In spring 1636, Hooker and approximately 100 of his parishioners moved to Hartford. They survived the journey by drinking milk from their cows and eating food given to them by the friendly Indians they met along the way. They arrived in good spirits, and the seeds of the colony of Connecticut had been planted.

In addition to the settlements at Windsor, Wethersfield, and Hartford, a fourth English settlement was started in 1635 at the mouth of the Connecticut River. It was called Saybrook and was established by a group of wealthy Puritans in England, although George Fenwick was the only member of the group to actually come from England. The fort that he and his men erected was intended as a trading post rather than a community like those upriver. By 1636, Plymouth, Massachusetts, New Netherland,

and the Saybrook colony all had conflicting claims along the Connecticut River.

CREATING THE COLONY OF CONNECTICUT

Although the Dutch arrived first, the small contingent of soldiers and traders at the House of Hope was no match for the growing number of English settlers. At this point, land a group could settle and defend was much more important than any existing legal claims. The Dutch lacked the number of colonists needed to hold onto their land claims. They lost part of their claim along the Delaware River and Bay to Sweden. They were also pushed out of the Connecticut River valley by settlers from Plymouth and

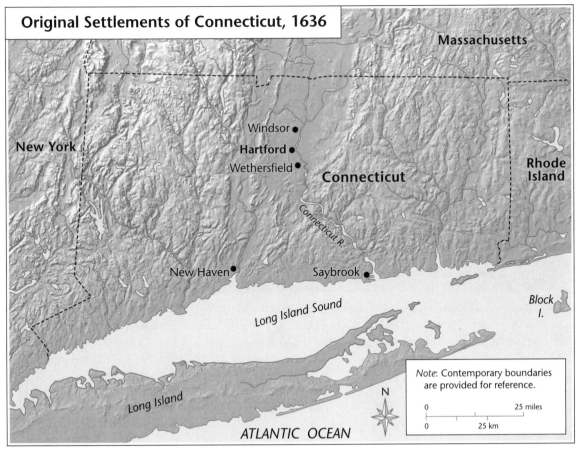

Original Settlements of Connecticut, 1636

Note: Contemporary boundaries are provided for reference.

The five original towns in Connecticut were actually three colonies. Windsor, Hartford, and Wethersfield were part of Connecticut Colony. New Haven and Saybrook were separate colonies.

Reverend John Davenport and some followers founded the Colony of New Haven in 1638 because they wanted to live more strictly than the Puritans in Boston. In this illustration, the New Haven Puritans celebrate their first Sunday in their new colony. *(North Wind Picture Archives)*

Massachusetts Bay Colonies. Eventually they had to give up all of New Netherland to the English.

Even though the Dutch were not a serious threat to the growing towns along the Connecticut River, there were still three different factions involved. Both Plymouth and Massachusetts Bay

Colonies claimed the area, as did the group who established Saybrook. To solve these conflicting claims, the General Court of Massachusetts set up an eight-member commission in March 1636 to oversee the settlements along the Connecticut River and settle any disputes that might arise.

The three towns of Windsor, Wethersfield, and Hartford banded together to form a single government. They set up an assembly that consisted of two magistrates and two deputies from each town. It was called the Connecticut General Court, and it met for the first time in April 1636. After three years without any written laws, the General Court decided to write down a code of laws. This document is known as the Fundamental Orders of Connecticut and is considered to be the first written constitution in the Western Hemisphere. In some ways, it would serve as a model for all the colonial and state constitutions that followed. Some contend that its impact can be seen in the U.S. Constitution. Many believe that Connecticut's present-day nickname "The Constitution State" came from this early constitution. Others believe the nickname came later when delegates from Connecticut were instrumental in creating the national constitution.

With the adoption of the Fundamental Orders on January 14, 1639, the three upriver towns were considered the colony of Connecticut. Saybrook continued to operate as a separate colony. In addition, a third colony was started at the mouth of the Quinnipiac River in 1638. This colony was called New Haven and was led by a wealthy Puritan named Reverend John Davenport who had arrived in Boston, Massachusetts, in 1637. Davenport and his followers thought the Puritans in Boston were not strict enough in applying the religious laws that Puritans were supposed to follow.

Since the founders of New Haven included many wealthy merchants and businessmen, the colony was quickly built up with substantial houses and laid out streets. The site was picked because it had a good harbor and was well situated to participate in trade with New Amsterdam to the south and Massachusetts to the north and had the Connecticut fur trade in its backyard.

The founders of the colony drew up their own set of rules known as the New Haven Fundamental Articles of 1639. Unlike the document created by the Connecticut Colony, New Haven's rules put the words of the Bible ahead of all else. Applying the laws of the Bible to the life of the colony was very attractive to many conservative Puritans. The New Haven colony grew rapidly. By 1643, it included New Haven and the surrounding towns of Branford, Fairfield, Greenwich, Guilford, Medford, Milford, and Stamford.

At this point, the area that is now Connecticut consisted of three colonies: the three upriver towns that were known as Connecticut, New Haven and its surrounding towns, and Saybrook. By 1640, there were almost 1,500 settlers in Connecticut, but in the years preceding this time, the entire area had been ravaged by warfare with the Pequot and their allies.

3

Conflicts with Native Americans

THE PEQUOT WAR

The Indians of Connecticut quickly found themselves in a difficult position. The Pequot had established themselves as the dominant tribe of the area and monopolized the trade with the Dutch. When English settlers from Massachusetts Bay and Plymouth Colonies started to move into the area many of the tribes along the Connecticut River welcomed them. The English at first paid the Indians for the land they took and gave the river tribes an outlet for their furs. Some of the Pequot also wanted to conduct business with the English, while others wished to maintain their trading alliance with the Dutch.

In 1631, Sassacus became the sachem (leader) of the Pequot. His son-in-law, Uncas, opposed him on the trade issue. The two leaders often argued during tribal councils, and their followers began to raid the trading partners of the other side. In 1633, Uncas and his people broke off from the Pequot and started a new community near present-day Lyme, Connecticut. They called themselves the Mohegan, which meant "wolf" in the Pequot language. Uncas was a member of the wolf clan and chose that name for his new tribe.

The situation for the Pequot worsened when smallpox epidemics killed many tribal members in the winters of 1633 and 1634. While Uncas and the Mohegan tried to remain allies of the

Native Americans and Disease

Most scholars agree that the ancestors of the Native Americans originated in Asia and traveled to North America when the two continents were connected by a land bridge between modern-day Siberia and Alaska. During the thousands of years they were isolated from the Asian and European continents, they lost or never developed any immunity to the diseases that the Europeans brought with them to North America.

Common diseases for Europeans like mumps and measles were often fatal for Native Americans. The most deadly disease, which had also killed large numbers of people in Europe, was smallpox. Smallpox epidemics ran through the Native American population of Connecticut numerous times during the colonial period. Very few Native Americans survived smallpox.

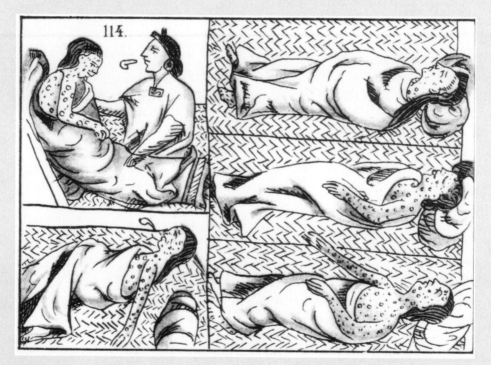

Published in *Historia general de las cosas de Nueva España* in the 1570s, this illustration shows Aztec people sick with smallpox. American Indians suffered great losses from the influx of European diseases that accompanied colonization. *(Library of Congress)*

English, the Pequot tried to stop English expansion in Connecticut. To make matters worse, in 1634, John Stone, a less than reputable English trader, was killed by Indians who were either Pequot or from a tribe that was allied with them. Stone had been attempting to capture Indians to sell into slavery when he was killed.

To prevent an all-out war, Sassacus went to Boston to talk to the leaders there. The officials in Boston wanted only one thing from Sassacus and that was the people who had killed Stone. Sassacus refused and went home angry. The English did not understand nor were they interested in the way the Pequot and other Indians dealt with crimes. Whoever killed Stone most likely thought it was acceptable since he was trying to capture American Indians to sell as slaves. In the thinking of the Puritans, non-Christian Indians were not entitled to any rights. The Puritans believed that it was God's will for them to make New England theirs. The actions of the Massachusetts leaders soon made their position completely clear.

In 1636, John Oldham, the Massachusetts trader who had helped establish the English community of Wethersfield, was killed while sailing near Block Island. His death was blamed on the Indians of the island who were allied with the Pequot. A force was quickly raised in Massachusetts and sent to Block Island under the leadership of John Endecott. There they killed 14 Indian men and burned the village and its surrounding fields. They then sailed to the Pequot territory on the mainland, where they attacked a Pequot village. This set off what is called the Pequot War.

In retaliation, the Pequot attacked the fort at Saybrook in September 1636 and February 1637. When reinforcements arrived at the fort, the Pequot turned their anger on the community of Wethersfield. In April 1637, a Pequot war party attacked a number of English settlers working in a field. They killed nine men and took two women as prisoners. The Connecticut General Court decided the time for action had come.

The court voted to place Captain John Mason in charge of a force of almost 100 men from the three Connecticut towns. A large group of Indians joined them. These were warriors from the river tribes, the Narragansett in Rhode Island, and about 60

An expedition led by John Endecott attacked Narragansett villages on Block Island in 1636 during the Pequot War. *(North Wind Picture Archives)*

Mohegan. On May 26, 1637, this large force approached the Pequot village near present-day Mystic, Connecticut. At dawn, they set the village on fire. Then setting up two rings of fighters around the perimeter of the village they shot those trying to flee the flames. Those who did not die in the fire were killed as they tried to flee. Most of the Pequot warriors were away on a raid, and it is estimated that as many as 700 people died in the village. Most of those who died were women, children, and men too old to fight.

During June 1637, the English force and their Indian allies hunted down the remaining Pequot. The warriors who were not killed in battle were often executed. Many of the women and children who were captured were given as slaves to the Indians fighting with the English or sent to slave markets in the Caribbean. Those who were not killed or captured left the area.

Sassacus and some of his remaining warriors went west to the lands of the Iroquois. When they entered a Mohawk village in what is now New York, they were killed before they were even allowed to state their case. The Pequot had been enemies of the Mohawk in the past. The Mohawk were not happy to see Sassacus and killed him before he even got a chance to speak to their council. To show

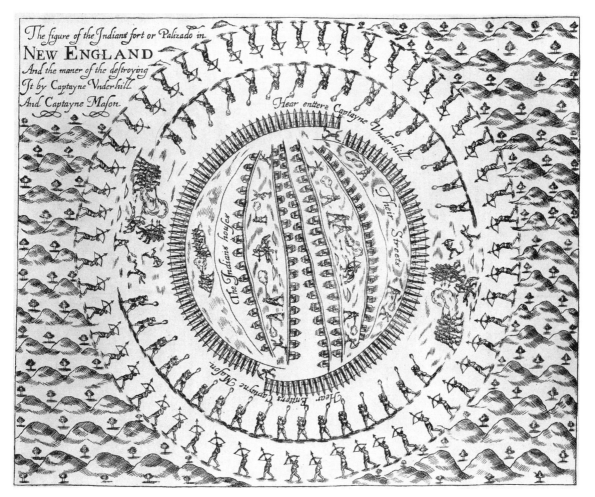

First published in a 1638 book, this illustration depicts the Pequot village that a colonial army led by Captains John Underhill and John Mason attacked in 1637. *(Library of Congress, Prints and Photographs Division [LC-USZ62-32055])*

the English colonists that they were not giving any aid to the Pequot, the Mohawk cut off Sassacus's head and sent it to Hartford. The elimination of the Pequot made it clear to all the Indians of the area that the English could be a ruthless enemy. The relative peace that followed the Pequot War attracted many additional settlers to the colonies of Connecticut, Saybrook, and New Haven. The English population of what is now Connecticut continued to grow.

NEW ENGLAND CONFEDERATION

Despite the time of peace that followed the Pequot War, the English colonists were still concerned about possible future attacks by Indians. By 1643, there were a number of English colonies in New England, each with its own government. Massachusetts Bay

Disagreements, which sometimes developed into wars between colonists and American Indians in the thirteen colonies, occurred often. In this illustration, Governor William Kieft, ruler of New Netherland from 1638 until 1647, leads Dutch forces against American Indians in 1644. *(North Wind Picture Archives)*

was the largest, but Plymouth was still a separate colony. Connecticut and Rhode Island had been established along with a colony at New Haven that would later become part of Connecticut. All of these colonies shared concerns about conflicts with their Indian neighbors.

The colonies needed more and more land to support their fast-growing populations. Sometimes treaties were made where the tribes were paid for the loss of their land. However, many times colonists took any land that they wanted. Realizing that additional conflicts were likely, the leaders of the New England colonies decided to form an alliance for their protection.

The colonies agreed to help defend each other and in 1643 formed the New England Confederation. Although the confederation lasted for more than 40 years, there was often rivalry among the colonies. The leaders of Massachusetts Bay thought they should have more of a say because their colony was by far the largest. The others thought each colony should be represented equally. This is an argument that would continue in one way or another until the U.S. Constitution was adopted.

The New England Confederation clearly recognized the independence of its members in the running of their colonies. What they agreed to do was to help each other in military matters. In 1675, the New England Confederation was put to its most serious test.

KING PHILLIP'S WAR

By 1670, there were more than 50,000 white people in New England, whereas 50 years earlier there had been none. Their settlements stretched along the coast from what is now Maine to the border between Connecticut and New York. From Connecticut, colonists had moved up the Connecticut River valley into western Massachusetts. This rapid population growth created a great deal of tension in New England.

Primary among these tensions was the colonists' need for land. The Indian tribes who inhabited the land before the arrival of the English obviously had first claim to it. However, England claimed the whole area as part of its empire. This was also complicated by border disputes between the colonies of Massachusetts Bay, Plymouth, Rhode Island, and Connecticut. Along the frontiers of the

Metacom, or King Phillip, became chief of the Wampanoag in 1662. *(Library of Congress, Prints and Photographs Division [LC-USZ62-96234])*

colonies, settlers often just took what they wanted and defended it as best they could.

In addition to the colonists' greed for more and more of the lands claimed by the various tribes in New England, there was an underlying racial intolerance on the part of the English colonists. Even Native Americans who had been converted to Christianity, called "Praying Indians" at the time, who fought alongside the colonists were treated as inferior citizens.

King Phillip's War was the unavoidable outcome of this conflict between cultures. Metacom, also called Metacomet, or King Phillip as the English called him, was the leader of the Wampanoag. He was the second son of Massasoit, the Wampanoag leader who had befriended and helped the Pilgrims at Plymouth. His story and the account of the rebellion he led against the white colonists of New England shows the roots of the mistreatment of Native Americans that continues to this day.

Unlike Massasoit, his sons saw the colonists as a threat on many levels. The colonists continued to take Wampanoag land and fought among themselves over who had the right to control the sale of Native American lands. After Massasoit died, his eldest son, Wamsutta, became the leader, or sachem, of the Wampanoag. As the leader of the tribe, he negotiated land sales to Rhode Island. Under the leadership of Roger Williams, Rhode Island probably had the best relationship of all the colonies with its Native American neighbors.

The leaders of Plymouth Colony did not want to see Rhode Island gain more land, especially where it encroached on lands that they claimed. Plymouth sent a small force led by Major Josiah Wilson to retrieve Wamsutta and bring him to Plymouth, where they planned to convince him to sell land only to them. During his captivity in Plymouth, Wamsutta became sick, and he died on his way home.

On the death of Wamsutta, Metacom became the leader of the Wampanoag. He was angered over the death of his brother, believing that Wamsutta had been poisoned by his captors. Metacom entered into a plot to drive the colonists back into the sea from which they came. He sent representatives to tribes throughout the area hoping to build a coalition of Native Americans. In January 1675, the rumors of a Native American uprising became believable for the colonists when a Praying Indian named John Sassamon reported to the governor of Plymouth Colony, Josiah Winslow, that Metacom was preparing for war.

After reporting to Governor Winslow, Sassamon was murdered. Metacom denied having any part in the murder. However, three Native Americans were captured, charged with the crime, and executed. Throughout the remainder of winter 1675, Wampanoag, Pocumtuc, and Nipmuck warriors attacked small settlements around the colonies. The outlying settlements, especially those in western Massachusetts in the Connecticut River Valley, felt the brunt of the early stages of the war.

In the meantime, the colonies had forced the Narragansett to sign a treaty in which they agreed to turn over all Wampanoag who might seek refuge with the Narragansett. In December 1675, Governor Winslow led a large force from Massachusetts and Connecticut into Narragansett territory to make sure they were not harboring any Wampanoag. Without further negotiation or proof that the Narragansett had violated the treaty, Winslow's forces began burning Narragansett villages. On December 19, 1675, Winslow reached the Narragansett's main village, which sat on high ground in the middle of the Great Swamp, near the current town of West Kingston, Rhode Island.

Normally this village was a well-defended spot surrounded by water. However, the winter of 1675–76 had already been a cold one and the colonists' forces were able to reach the village by

Originally published in *Harper's New Monthly Magazine* in 1857 and quite partial to the colonists involved in the incident, this engraving illustrates the colonists' defeat of a Narragansett village in the Great Swamp of Rhode Island in December 1675. *(Library of Congress, Prints and Photographs Division [LC-USZ62-97115])*

crossing the frozen swamp. It has been estimated that 300 Narragansett warriors and an equal number of women and children were killed on that day. There was no evidence then or now that the Narragansett were ever allied with Metacom. The guerilla warfare of the Native Americans was met with large forces of colonists and their "Praying Indian" allies killing any Native Americans they could find.

It soon became obvious that King Phillip's War was going to end the Native Americans' hopes of hanging on to any power in New England. Metacom was betrayed, and the colonists, along with their Native American allies, trapped him in a swamp near New Hope, Rhode Island. When Metacom's body was finally found among the fallen, the colonial commander, Captain Church, ordered that Metacom be decapitated and the remainder of his body cut in quarters. The head was returned to Plymouth, where it was put on public display.

In the end, more than 5,000 Native Americans and 2,500 colonists died during King Phillip's War. Many captured Native Americans were transported to the Caribbean and sold as slaves. It has been estimated that these numbers represented 40 percent of the Native Americans and 5 percent of the whites in New England at the time. If that is the case, King Phillip's War was the bloodiest ever fought by North Americans. From that point forward, the relations with Native Americans involved sending in the military first and then making peace with the survivors—if there were any. However, ending any possible threat to the colonies from Native Americans was not the end of the problems the colonies faced.

Revolution and Restoration in England

Even before the colonies of Connecticut and New Haven were established, Charles I, the king of England, was having problems at home. In 1629, Charles dissolved the English Parliament when it refused to give him the resources he needed to fight a war with Scotland. There were a number of Puritans in Parliament, including John Winthrop who led many Puritans to New England. The Puritans also objected to Charles's plans for the Church of England. Many refer to this time as the "Great Migration" because thousands of Puritan and non-Puritan English people fled the chaos in England for the American colonies.

Charles I recalled Parliament in 1640, only to dismiss it after just three weeks. Later that year, Charles I recalled Parliament again. This Parliament would stay in session for the next 13 years, during one of the darkest times in modern English history. The Puritans in Parliament and throughout the country rose up against Charles I, and a civil war began in 1642.

The Puritans in the English Civil War were called "Roundheads" because they wore their hair in a close cropped fashion that was in keeping with the simple dress that the Puritans adopted. The king's followers wore their hair long and were referred to as *Cavaliers*, a term that had been used in the past to describe mounted knights.

Oliver Cromwell rose to the top of the Puritan army and proved to be a very capable military leader. His "New Model Army" won a number of victories and eventually defeated the king's forces.

Charles I was tried and then executed for treason on January 30, 1649. After defeating the Catholic and royalist forces in Ireland and Scotland, Oliver Cromwell became the Lord Protector of England. During the English Civil War, the colonies had been left alone to develop ways of governing themselves. Each of the Connecticut colonies developed their own forms of government.

After the Puritan victory in England, there was a period of reverse migration, when large numbers of people went back to England to be a part of the Puritan country that was being created. Many leaders in New England were concerned that England would become the place of Puritan power and would affect the way they lived and worshipped.

In England, Cromwell and his advisers saw that trade with the colonies in North America had suffered. Due to the turmoil of the English Civil War and the disruption in trade that it caused, many traders in North America and especially those in New England had begun trading with the French and the Dutch in the Caribbean and Europe.

Oliver Cromwell was a Puritan and military leader who eventually became Lord Protector of England. *(Library of Congress, Prints and Photographs Division [LC-USZ62-95711])*

To bring trade with the colonies back under control of England, Parliament passed the first Navigation Acts in 1651. The part of this law that most affected the merchants of New England stated that colonies could only trade with England.

Many believe that the Navigation Acts of 1651, as well as the additions to them over the next 40 years, had two consequences. First, some merchants continued to trade as they had, in defiance of the English laws. Other merchants obeyed the laws but thought they were unfair. Although the importance of the Navigation Acts in eventually bringing about the American Revolution is probably minimal, they did contribute to a sense of defiance toward England.

Although Cromwell's victories were in part a victory for the rising middle classes in England, the country was not ready for the strict ideals of the Puritans. When Cromwell died in 1658, his son took over as Lord Protector. He lasted only nine months in the job before he resigned and a battle began to restore Charles II, Charles I's son, to the throne.

After a number of battles, Charles II's forces prevailed, and the monarchy was restored. Charles II ruled as king of England, Scotland, and Ireland for the next 25 years. At the restoration of the monarchy, many Puritans fled to the colonies. This was a period of relative stability in England, and the king and his ministers were able to devote some of their attention to the English colonies in North America. After years of benign neglect, Charles II wanted to assert his control over what he saw as English territory.

Many in England were concerned about the growing independence of Massachusetts Colony. To take away much of the local authority, Charles II revoked the Massachusetts charter. At the same time Maine and New Hampshire became separate colonies. The leaders in Connecticut saw this as a chance to strengthen their own

Excerpt from the Navigation Acts of 1651

"For the increase of the shipping and the encouragement of the navigation of this nation, which under the good providence and protection of God is so great a means of the welfare and safety of this Commonwealth: be it enacted by this present Parliament, and the authority thereof, that from and after the first day of December, one thousand six hundred fifty and one, and from thence forwards, no goods or commodities whatsoever of the growth, production or manufacture of Asia, Africa or America, or of any part thereof; or of any islands belonging to them, or which are described or laid down in the usual maps or cards of those places, as well of the English plantations as others, shall be imported or brought into this Commonwealth of England, or into Ireland, or any other lands, islands, plantations, or territories to this Commonwealth belonging, or in their possession, in any other ship or ships, vessel or vessels whatsoever, but only in such as do truly and without fraud belong only to the people of this Commonwealth, or the plantations thereof, as the proprietors or right owners thereof; and whereof the master and mariners are also for the most part of them of the people of this Commonwealth, under the penalty of the forfeiture and loss of all the goods that shall be imported contrary to this act; as also of the ship (with all her tackle, guns and apparel) in which the said goods or commodities shall be so brought in and imported; the one moiety to the use of the Commonwealth, and the other moiety to the use and behoof of any person or persons who shall seize the goods or commodities, and shall prosecute the same in any court of record within this Commonwealth."

Charles II
(1630–1685)

Charles II was 19 years old when his father was executed in 1649. Charles, his brother James, and many of his father's supporters were forced to leave England. Scotland and parts of Ireland recognized him as king, and in 1651 he invaded England from Scotland with an army of 10,000 men. As Charles made his way south, people turned out to greet his army and proclaim him king. However, on September 3, 1651, Charles's army was defeated by Oliver Cromwell in a battle near the English town of Worcester.

Charles fled to France where he lived in poverty until he returned as king after a royalist army defeated the Puritans. Before he could take the throne, he was forced to give more power to Parliament. Charles II ruled from 1660 until his death in 1685. During his reign, life in England was relatively calm; however, Charles was constantly in need of money to support his lavish lifestyle as king. He may have been trying to make up for the years he had lived in poverty in exile.

colony by getting a charter from the king. John Winthrop, Jr., who was governor at the time, sailed to England in 1661 in the hope of getting a charter for the colony.

Winthrop did better than anyone expected. The king gave Connecticut a charter on April 23, 1662, that allowed for some local control and added the New Haven Colony to Connecticut. The big surprise was the boundaries of the royal colony of Connecticut. The northern and southern boundaries described in the charter were almost the same as the current boundaries of the state of Connecticut. However, Narragansett Bay became the eastern boundary of Connecticut, which put most of Rhode Island in Connecticut. Even more surprising was the western boundary: the Pacific Ocean.

Although people from Connecticut would later try to claim a strip of land in Pennsylvania,

Charles II ruled England, Scotland, and Ireland from 1660 until his death in 1685. *(Library of Congress, Prints and Photographs Division [LC-USZ62-96910])*

over the years their claims to land outside of what is now Connecticut were negotiated away to the surrounding colonies and later states. The biggest problem under the new charter was the fact that New Haven was to become part of Connecticut. People from New Haven had gone to England in hopes of getting their own charter. When the people of New Haven heard about the loss of their colony, they were very angry. Some wanted to fight. Others talked about moving away so they could remain an independent colony.

Two years later in 1664, when Charles II gave his brother James the right to what was then New Netherland, the people of New Haven were glad to be a part of Connecticut. The land given to James included most of present-day New York, New Jersey, Delaware, and Connecticut. Although James's charter included most of Connecticut, he put most of his efforts into turning New Netherland into New York. The people of New Haven were much happier as part of Puritan Connecticut. They were given a say in their own government unlike in New York, where the royal governor was given most of the authority.

DOMINION OF NEW ENGLAND

After 25 years with Charles II as king, his brother, James II, a Catholic, became king of England in 1685. James's religion created numerous problems for him. He was king for only four years before he was overthrown. In that short time, he created havoc in the colonies as well as in England. He did not return Massachusetts Bay Colony's charter. Instead, he consolidated the New England colonies of Massachusetts, Maine, Plymouth, Rhode Island, and Connecticut into one colony called the Dominion of New England.

In December 1686, Sir Edmund Andros arrived in Boston to take up his post as royal governor of the Dominion of New England. By 1688, the Dominion of New England was expanded to include all of

Edmund Andros ruled the Dominion of New England as its royal governor. *(Published by George Burner, 1903)*

James, Duke of York and Albany, Later King James II
(1633–1701)

In 1649, King Charles I was removed from the throne and executed after a Puritan revolution in England. His two sons, Charles, Prince of Wales, and James, duke of York, were forced to spend the next eight years living in exile while the Puritan Oliver Cromwell ran England. Charles lived in poverty in the Netherlands, and James went to Spain, where he joined the Spanish navy in its war against Protestant England. When the English monarchy was restored in 1660, James's older brother became Charles II, king of England.

Charles II appointed James Lord High Admiral of the navy and in 1664 granted James all the lands between the Connecticut and Delaware Rivers in North America. James sent a fleet to capture the territory claimed by the Dutch and was involved with the fate of New York and New Jersey for the next 24 years.

In 1672, James created a controversy by revealing that he had converted to Catholicism. Although England tolerated many different Protestant sects, the country was not tolerant of Catholics. In fact, in 1673, Parliament passed a series of laws called the Tests Acts, which barred Catholics from holding office. James was forced to resign his position as Lord High Admiral.

Because his brother had not produced an heir, James was next in line to become king of England. On his brother's death in 1685, many tried to block James from becoming king. However, they were unsuccessful, and he became James II, king of England.

As king, he was faced with a number of uprisings in England. He was extremely brutal in addressing any resistance to his rule. He was so unpopular that, in 1688, he was removed from the throne in a bloodless coup known as the Glorious Revolution. After a brief and unsuccessful attempt to regain his throne, he spent the rest of his life living in exile in France.

James II ruled England for only four years. During that time, he combined Massachusetts, Maine, Plymouth, Connecticut, and Rhode Island to create the Dominion of New England. *(Library of Congress, Prints and Photographs Division [LC-USZ62-92123])*

New England, Nova Scotia to the north, and New York and New Jersey to the south. Part of the justification for the dominion was the growing conflict between the English colonies and the French colony in Canada. However, Andros ruled the Dominion of New England as a dictator backed up by troops he had brought from England.

The Charter Oak

When Governor Edmund Andros arrived in New England, he requested that the colonies give up their royal charters. On October 31, 1687, Governor Andros arrived in Hartford to collect Connecticut's charter. As he talked with members of the Connecticut government in the council room, the charter was on the table before them. The candles that lit the room suddenly went out and when they were relit, the charter was gone. Legend has it that the charter was taken out and hidden in a huge old, hollow oak. It is said that when Andros was removed from his position by the people of Massachusetts, leaders in Connecticut "found" the charter and restored it to its place in the council room. The oak it was supposedly hidden in was called the "charter oak." The charter oak stood in Hartford until August 1856, when it was blown down in a storm. People estimated that the charter oak was almost 1,000 years old.

THE CHARTER OAK.
Lith. of D.W. Kellogg & Co. Hartford, Ct.

The Charter Oak, a hollow oak tree in Hartford, Connecticut, that fell in 1856, is believed to be where leaders in Connecticut hid their royal charter when Edmund Andros tried to take it from them in 1687. *(The Connecticut Historical Society, Hartford, Connecticut)*

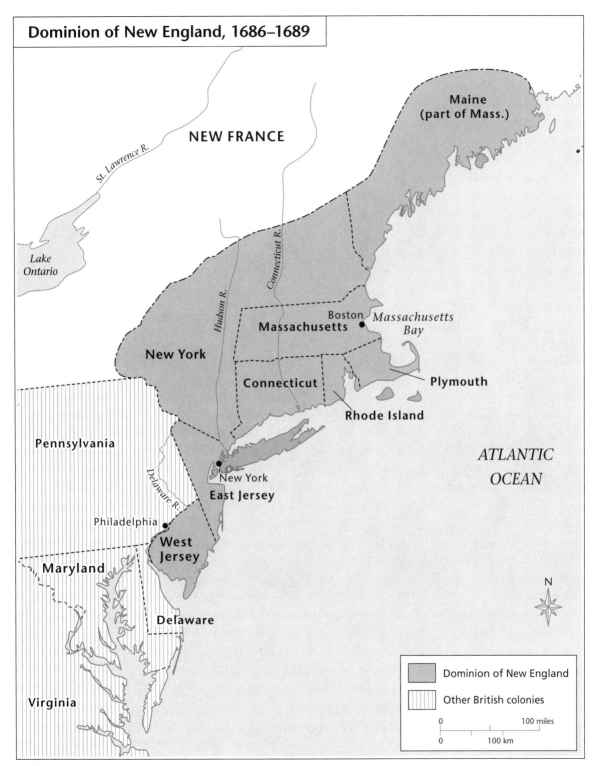

Dominion of New England, 1686–1689

St. Lawrence R.

NEW FRANCE

Maine
(part of Mass.)

Lake
Ontario

Hudson R.

Connecticut R.

Boston

Massachusetts
Bay

Massachusetts

Connecticut

Plymouth

Rhode Island

Pennsylvania

ATLANTIC
OCEAN

Delaware R.

New York

East Jersey

Philadelphia

West
Jersey

Maryland

Delaware

Virginia

N

Dominion of New England

Other British colonies

0   100 miles

0   100 km

When James II became king of England, he combined Connecticut Colony with a number of other colonies into one large colony known as the Dominion of New England.

William and Mary became the rulers of England, Scotland, and Ireland in what is known as the Glorious Revolution of 1688. *(Library of Congress, Prints and Photographs Division [LC-USZ62-87571])*

Andros suspended the colonial governments and set up his own courts. He also levied taxes on the colonists without their consent. In addition to political changes, Andros altered the Puritan nature of New England, angering many. He forced religious toleration on the colonies and favored the Church of England over the Puritan churches.

When it was learned that James II had been overthrown in a bloodless rebellion referred to as the Glorious Revolution, the colonists seized this opportunity to get rid of Andros. Andros had been on a military expedition to the frontier to defend the colonies against raids by Native Americans allied with the French in Canada. When he returned to Boston, the local population was in rebellion. A group had formed, calling itself the "Committee for the Safety of the People." In April 1689, Andros was arrested and put in Boston's jail by members of the committee. Elsewhere in the dominion, Andros's appointed leaders were also removed from office. Shortly thereafter, Andros and his staff were sent back to England and the Dominion of New England ended.

In the early days of the American Revolution, many colonists looked back on the overthrow of Edmund Andros as the first act in the long struggle for independence. This may be the case, but the changes affected by enforced religious tolerance and the rule of a royal governor greatly lessened the powers of the Puritan leaders of the colonies of New England.

5

The Growth of Connecticut

In 1640, there were fewer than 1,500 settlers in what would become the Colony of Connecticut. By 1760, there were more than 150,000 people in Connecticut, which gave it the fifth-largest population of the thirteen colonies. Although people came from all over Europe to live in the colonies, Connecticut residents were primarily of English origin. Many factors contributed to the growth of the colony. The land and climate of Connecticut helped its farmers prosper. Connecticut merchants were successful in trading goods, including items locally manufactured in Connecticut, produced in the colonies around the world. Connecticut also provided education for its residents, which was not the case in many colonies.

EDUCATION IN CONNECTICUT

Among the beliefs of the Puritans was the idea that the Bible provided a guide for living one's life. It was, therefore, important that all Puritans, both men and women be able to read and study the Bible. To make sure that the children of Connecticut got the opportunity to learn to read, Connecticut passed a law in 1650, which required every town with 50 or more people to have a school. These schools were supported by local taxes. Most of these schools had only one room and all the school-age children of the community went to school together. The older children often helped the younger ones with their lessons.

This house, built in Stonington, Connecticut, in 1700 by Robert Stanton, is an example of a home owned by a more wealthy Connecticut colonist. Stanton's parents, Thomas and Ann Stanton, were both born in England, met and married in the colony, and ran a tradinghouse in Stonington. *(Library of Congress, Prints and Photographs Division [HABS, CONN, 6-STONI, 4-2])*

At first, students in New England schools used what were called "hornbooks." These were not like modern schoolbooks. A hornbook consisted of a square of wood with a handle and a printed page attached to it. Over the printed page was a transparent sheet of horn made from a cow's horn. The pages had the alphabet, numbers, prayers, and other information on them. Students learned to write by tracing on the sheet of horn. In 1690, a new type of book was introduced into the schools of New England and soon became the standard textbook for most schools. It was called a primer and had much more information than the awkward hornbooks.

The New England Primer
(1690)

In 1690, Benjamin Harris, a Boston publisher and journalist who was born and educated in England, created a book called *The New England Primer*. The *Primer* included alphabets, lists of words, prayers, and poems. Almost all of the content had a religious tone, which reflected the Puritan attitudes of many of the people in New England. *The New England Primer* continued to be used in some schools into the 19th century. Even learning the alphabet became a religious exercise, as this excerpt from the 1777 edition of *The New England Primer* illustrates.

A Wise son maketh a glad father, but a foolish son is the heaviness of his mother.

Better is a little with the fear of the Lord, than great treasure & trouble therewith.

Come unto Christ all ye that labor and are heavy laden and he will give you rest.

Do not the abominable thing which I hate saith the Lord.

Except a man be born again, he cannot see the kingdom of God.

Foolishness is bound up in the heart of a child, but the rod of correction shall drive it far from him.

Godliness is profitable unto all things, having the promise of the life that now is, and that which is to come.

Holiness becomes GOD's house for ever.

Attendance at school was erratic. Children were often needed at home to help with chores on their families' farms. Many students stopped attending once they had mastered the basics of reading and writing. There were some schools where more extensive subjects were taught for students who might go on to become lawyers, ministers, doctors, or other professionals. A student who intended to go to college needed to learn Greek and Latin as well as the rudiments of history, geography, and other more advanced subjects.

In the early years of the Connecticut colonies, students who wanted to attend college traveled to Massachusetts, where Harvard College had been established in 1636. However, as the 18th century began there were almost 26,000 people in Connecticut. The General Assembly decided it was time for the colony to have its own college. Some in Connecticut who had pushed for a college of their own thought that Harvard had become too lax in the teaching of Puritan doctrine and wanted to establish a more conservative school. In 1701, the General Assembly voted to establish what at first was called the Collegiate School. In its first year, 1702, the Collegiate School had one student who studied at the home of Reverend Abraham Pierson in what is now Clinton, Connecticut. Ministers in Connecticut donated books to start the college's library.

The Collegiate School was the third college to be established in the colonies. Harvard in Massachusetts was first in 1636. The College of William and Mary opened its doors to the students of Virginia in 1693. After starting in Reverend Pierson's house, the Collegiate School moved twice before finally going to New Haven in 1716. The school was still on rocky ground financially when it first came to New Haven. However, in 1718, Elihu Yale, an English merchant who was born in Boston, donated a large amount of

Many children living in what would become the Colony of Connecticut attended school in one-room schoolhouses, earlier versions of the one shown here in Robertsville, Connecticut, in 1905. *(The Connecticut Historical Society, Hartford, Connecticut)*

Yale University, shown in an image dating to 1832, began in 1702 as the Collegiate School in Clinton, Connecticut, and moved twice before it was established in New Haven in 1716. *(Library of Congress, Prints and Photographs Division [LC-USZ62-51258])*

money to the Collegiate School. In that same year, the name of the school was changed to Yale College to honor its benefactor. In 1887, Yale became a university and is today recognized as one of the top universities in the world.

LIFE ON THE FARMS OF CONNECTICUT

The vast majority of people in Connecticut were farmers. After the land in the river valleys was settled, people began clearing the forests of Connecticut to have more land to farm. Although Connecticut has four distinct seasons and its winter storms can sometimes be harsh, the growing season was long enough for the colonists to grow many crops. Many early colonists started farming by planting Indian corn, but they were soon growing a number of English crops as well.

A typical farm during this time grew rye, oats, peas, squashes, corn, and a variety of other vegetables. In addition, most of the colonists grew flax. Flax stalks contain long thin fibers that can be spun into thread. The women on the farms wove the thread into a material known as linen. Clothing and bedding were often made of linen. In addition to growing crops, each farm raised a variety of animals. Cattle were kept for meat, and each farm had dairy cows for milk and making cheese and butter.

Chickens, for meat and eggs, were also kept, as were sheep, pigs, and horses. In early times, a team of oxen was likely to be the work animals on Connecticut farms. Sheep were very important to the farmers of Connecticut; some were slaughtered for their meat, but most were kept for their wool. Imported wool cloth from England was very expensive when it was available. Every farmhouse in Connecticut had its own spinning wheel and loom for making woolen cloth referred to as "homespun." With the possible exception of an outfit to wear to church on Sunday, almost all the farmers and their families wore clothes of wool and linen that were grown and processed on the farm.

Most Connecticut farmers were able to grow more than their own families needed. The excess farm produce of Connecticut was traded for manufactured goods. There was very little money in any of the colonies, so most business was done by barter. There were

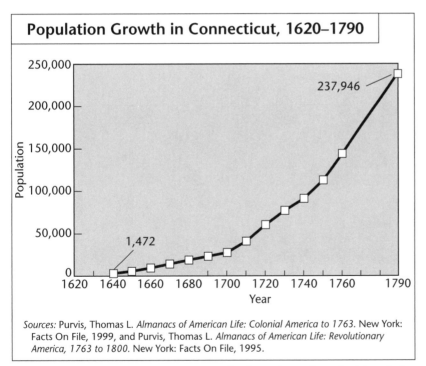

Population Growth in Connecticut, 1620–1790

Sources: Purvis, Thomas L. *Almanacs of American Life: Colonial America to 1763*. New York: Facts On File, 1999, and Purvis, Thomas L. *Almanacs of American Life: Revolutionary America, 1763 to 1800*. New York: Facts On File, 1995.

The population of Connecticut grew rapidly throughout the colonial period, making it the fifth largest colony.

Tobacco in Connecticut

One of the early cash crops for Connecticut farmers was tobacco. This was a plant the local Indians grew to smoke in pipes during their religious ceremonies. Smoking tobacco was introduced into Europe by Christopher Columbus and demand for the smokable leaves of the plant increased quickly. Connecticut farmers, however, could not compete with the large plantations that grew tobacco in the colonies of Maryland, Virginia, and North Carolina and most gave up growing tobacco as a crop.

Later, the Connecticut river valley became a place where a special type of tobacco was cultivated. This tobacco is still grown in fields that are covered with nets to provide shade. "Shade-grown" tobacco is valued because it is used for the outer wrapper of cigars.

Early in Connecticut's colonial history, farmers cultivated tobacco but often found they could not compete with plantations in Maryland, Virginia, and North Carolina. Some men and boys pose in a field of tobacco plants in Hartford County, Connecticut, in an early 1900s photograph. *(The Connecticut Historical Society, Hartford, Connecticut)*

Farms were integral to life in colonial Connecticut. In this 1880s photograph, a family works on their tobacco farm in Westchester, Connecticut. *(The Connecticut Historical Society, Hartford, Connecticut)*

few stores in rural Connecticut, and many of the farms were visited by traveling merchants who came to be known as "Yankee peddlers." A Yankee peddler would arrive at a farm with a wide variety of goods in his wagon—everything from pots, pans, buttons, thread, and cloth to rifles and ammunition. The farmers bargained for these goods by offering whatever they might have in excess. Many farmers also hunted and trapped and might have had furs or deerskins to trade.

The workday on a colonial Connecticut farm began when the sun came up and continued until it was too dark to work outside, and then work went on inside. As soon as the children of the family were big enough, they were expected to help in any way they could. This might include taking care of their younger brothers and sisters as well as helping out with the work around

Saybrook Platform
(1708)

The Congregational churches of Connecticut and the rest of New England were under the control of each group of local parishioners. In 1708, the church leaders of Connecticut met in Saybrook and came up with a plan to oversee the independent churches of Connecticut. The document they produced is called the Saybrook Platform. In essence, it is a constitution for running the Congregational churches in Connecticut. Each church maintained a certain amount of independence but had to go along with the rules of the church leaders.

the farm. In colonial times, there was a strict division of labor between the sexes. In addition, the laws of the time recognized the husband as the head of the household in all matters.

Women and girls spent their time caring for children, cooking, and possibly taking care of a small vegetable garden. They might also feed the chickens and milk the cows. In the winter when there was less outside work to do, the females of the household spent much of their time spinning, weaving, and making clothes for their family. The men and able boys did the majority of the heavy work of farming. Plowing, planting, and harvesting took up much of their time. Tending the pigs, cattle, sheep, and horses was also time-consuming, especially considering that all the winter feed for the livestock had to be grown on the farm and stored in the barn.

Working hard was part of the Puritan ethic, and many of those who followed this ethic became successful farmers in Connecticut. Six days a week, everyone on the farm worked long, hard hours. At sundown on Saturday, all work ceased except for feeding livestock, which always had to be done. Sunday was the day of worship, and most of Connecticut's farmers and other residents spent at least half the day at church. They listened to a sermon that might last for two hours and then spent the rest of the morning singing hymns and saying prayers. During the 17th century, the Puritans began to refer to themselves as *Congregationalists*. This term was used because each congregation had a certain amount of say in the conduct of its local church. The Congregational Church still exists in New England and elsewhere.

COMMERCE IN CONNECTICUT

Although Connecticut did not have a large port like Boston or New York City, the many towns along the coast and Hartford, which could be reached by ships sailing up the Connecticut River, prospered through trade. Some of the early merchants in Connecticut, as well as elsewhere in New England, became wealthy by loading their ships with excess lumber and food produced in the colony and trading it in the large cities of Boston and New York. Soon Connecticut ships were sailing farther and farther away.

Trade with the plantations of the Caribbean was especially lucrative. These large estates were too busy growing sugar to raise food for the many slaves they had working their plantations. It was more profitable for them to trade sugar for food and the other goods they needed. Much of the sugar that was acquired in the Caribbean was brought back to Connecticut where it was distilled into rum. Rum became one of the major exports of New England and was also consumed by the colonists. Although the Puritans did not tolerate public drunkenness, many people drank hard cider or

Slavery in Connecticut

In 1760, it is estimated that about 3 percent of the population or fewer than 4,000 people of African descent lived in Connecticut. It is assumed that most of these were slaves. In colonies that had large plantations like Virginia and South Carolina, slavery became an important part of the economy. In 1760, Virginia's population was over 40 percent black, while in South Carolina blacks were more than half (60 percent) of the population. Although some large farms may have had a few slaves to help work their fields, the majority of the slaves in Connecticut and elsewhere in New England, ended up as servants in the homes of the wealthy. Some Connecticut merchants most likely were involved in transporting slaves, although it was not a major part of the economy as it was for merchants in nearby Rhode Island.

Norwich, and New Haven—all had populations of between 5,000 and 6,000. At this time, the government of the colony still split its time between two capitals: New Haven and Hartford. The colony did not even have a newspaper until 1755, when the *Connecticut Gazette* was established in New Haven by James Parker. Although Connecti-

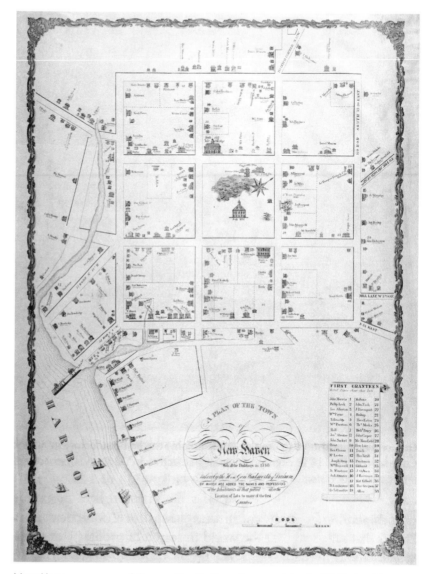

New Haven was one of Connecticut's three largest cities in 1760. In this 1748 drawing, the plan for New Haven is clearly visible. *(Beinecke Rare Book and Manuscript Library, Yale University)*

The *Connecticut Gazette* was Connecticut's first newspaper. Shown here is the front page of the first issue, which was published on April 12, 1755. *(Beinecke Rare Book and Manuscript Library, Yale University)*

cut remained a relatively safe and peaceful place after King Phillip's War, soldiers from Connecticut participated in a number of campaigns during the four French and Indian wars that were fought in North America between 1689 and 1762.

6

Colonial Wars

France and England were the two strongest countries in Europe and competed around the world for trade and colonies. Between 1689 and 1762, the two countries fought four wars. The wars often spilled over into other parts of the world where both countries had colonies. In North America, the French had numerous Indian allies who raided settlements along the borders between the English colonies and New France in what is now Canada. Although these wars had different names in Europe, in the English colonies they were known as: King William's War (1689–97); Queen Anne's War (1702–13); King George's War (1744–48); and the French and Indian War (1754–62).

During these wars, there was no fighting in Connecticut. However, militia from Connecticut went to fight in a number of campaigns, especially those in neighboring Massachusetts and New York. The wars also caused some conflict between the colonies. During the first war, the royal governor of New York, Benjamin Fletcher, was faced with numerous attacks in the northern part of his colony. Fletcher was given permission by the king to take charge of the Connecticut militia to help defend New York. This created a serious problem.

It was not that people in Connecticut did not want to help their neighbors in New York. They were upset that the governor of New York was going to have command over soldiers from Connecticut. On October 26, 1693, Governor Fletcher arrived in Hartford to take

William Shirley served as governor of Massachusetts from 1741 to 1756.
(Library of Congress, Prints and Photographs Division [LC-USZ62-85100])

over the Connecticut forces. When his aide began to read the governor's orders, Connecticut captain Joseph Wadsworth signaled his drummers to start beating their drums. Fletcher got the drummers to stop a couple of times, but as soon as his aide began to read again the drummers drowned out his words so none of the men could hear them.

After several attempts to stop the drummers by Fletcher, Wadsworth reportedly threatened to shoot Fletcher if he interrupted the drummers again. Fletcher returned to New York, and Connecticut sent a representative to England to petition the king to prevent officials from other colonies from interfering in Connecticut again. In part to prove the point that this incident was not about the war but about politics, Connecticut sent 120 men to New York to help fight the French and their Indian allies.

During Queen Anne's War, Connecticut forces helped English and other colonial forces capture Port Royal, Nova Scotia. After this war, England gained control of Nova Scotia, but the French kept the large island of Cape Breton, located northeast of the mainland. At Louisbourg on Cape Breton, the French proceeded to fortify the harbor with a huge fort and outlying artillery batteries. Louisbourg served as a safe harbor for French shipping and as a protector of the entrance to the St. Lawrence River.

When fighting broke out during King George's War, the French at Louisbourg decided to attack Nova Scotia. They easily captured the fishing village of Canso. In fact, when confronted by the large French force, the small garrison negotiated for their surrender. The major concession they wanted was to be transported to Boston instead of becoming French prisoners. The French agreed but took them to Louisbourg first.

When the prisoners finally arrived in Boston, the people of New England were extremely upset by their reports of French aggression. The Massachusetts governor, William Shirley, called a secret session of the Massachusetts assembly and proposed an attack on Louisbourg using the intelligence gathered from the recently arrived captives. At first, Shirley's plan was rejected. However, when news leaked out that the legislature had denied Shirley's plan, there was such an uproar in Boston that the legislature reconsidered and plans were made to attack Louisbourg.

Governor Shirley wrote to England requesting help from the English fleet in the Caribbean that was commanded by Commodore Peter Warren. In spring 1745, a force was assembled. It consisted of 3,000 volunteer militia from Massachusetts, 450 from New Hampshire, and 500 from Connecticut. The leader of the Connecticut troops was Lieutenant Governor Roger Wolcott. Other colonies provided supplies, ships, and cannons for the expedition. As commander, Shirley selected William Pepperell, who was the president of the Massachusetts legislature, a colonel in the militia, and a successful merchant from Kittery in the district of Maine.

When Pepperell left Boston, he had 4,000 militia under his command, 15 armed ships, and more than 100 transports. The forces were to meet in Canso before attacking Louisbourg. On April 23, 1745, Commodore Warren sailed into Canso in command of a 60-gun ship with two 40-gun ships as part of his squadron. On the 29th, they all sailed the short distance to Louisbourg. However, they did not attack directly. Instead, they entered the large bay to the southwest of the fortress, out of range of its guns.

It would have been foolish to directly attack the fort. Instead, Pepperell landed his forces and then moved behind the

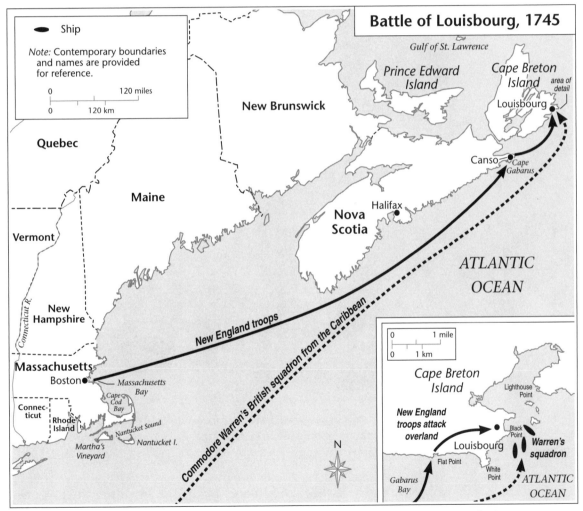

During King George's War, 500 Connecticut soldiers helped a force of soldiers from the colonies to capture the French fort at Louisbourg on Cape Breton Island, Nova Scotia.

Under the command of William Pepperell, a volunteer militia with members from Massachusetts, Connecticut, and New Hampshire defeated the French at Louisbourg, Cape Breton Island. Sailors and ship captains from Rhode Island provided transportation. *(Library of Congress, Prints and Photographs Division [LC-USZ62-105732])*

town where they could bombard it. The fortifications had been designed to protect the harbor, and the fort's big guns could not be swung around to fire on the colonial militia. With the colo-

nials attacking from the rear and Warren preventing any ships from entering or leaving the harbor, the undermanned garrison eventually surrendered. The greatest fortress in North America was captured with just over 100 deaths for the colonials.

However, the campaign was not without its problems. Many men were left behind to maintain the fortress and hold it against the French, but by spring 1746, almost 900 of them had died of disease. The French mounted two attempts to recapture Louisbourg but never fired a shot. The first fleet was sent back to France by a series of storms in the Atlantic Ocean. The second fleet was ravaged by an epidemic before it encountered a British fleet and was defeated.

The Battle of Louisbourg was a victory that made many in the colonies feel proud. They had done their part to help secure their corner of the world. They also had done service to the cause of England. It was with much dismay and anger that the people of New England who had lent support greeted the news of the Treaty of Aix-la-Chapelle. In the treaty, which ended King George's War, the English traded Louisbourg back to the French for control of the colony of Madras in India. The king agreed to reimburse the colonies for the cost of capturing Louisbourg, which only partly soothed the colonials' anger. Despite peace in Europe, fighting continued along the frontier as both the English and French colonies tried to expand their borders. It was these border conflicts that once again threw France and England into war.

THE FRENCH AND INDIAN WAR

The first three French and Indian wars had started in Europe and then spilled over to the French and English colonies. The final conflict between France and England in North America is known as the French and Indian War. It started in North America and then spread to all the corners of the world where France and England had colonies, as well as to Europe. The war started in 1754 in the Ohio River valley where the French came in conflict with English colonists from Virginia and Pennsylvania.

Unlike previous conflicts, large numbers of British regular troops were sent to the colonies to attack the French and finally settle the question of who would control North America. Many members of the colonial militia fought with the regular army. Connecticut did its share by providing over 5,000 militia who fought in upstate New York and in Canada when both Quebec and Montreal were captured. Israel Putnam, who became one of the leading American generals during the Revolution, was one of Connecticut's militia leaders in the French and Indian War. He was best known for being a member of Rogers's Rangers, a special force of colonial fighters.

Many Connecticut ships were involved in the French and Indian War, and many merchants added substantially to their fortunes by supplying the British forces. A number of colonial ships were hired as transport for the British forces, while other ship captains were given letters of marque. These letters gave them a legal right to attack enemy shipping.

A ship that was operating under a letter of marque was referred to as a privateer. When the colonies began the War for Independence, privateers were the only naval force they had. Many colonial soldiers gained experience during the French and Indian War that was of great value when it came time to fight for independence just 12 years after the end of the war.

When the Treaty of Paris was signed in 1763, France gave up its claims in North America with the exception of two small islands at the mouth of the St. Lawrence River. The islands of St.

Rogers's Rangers

Militia from New England joined with the British regulars in the fight against the French and their Native American allies. It was in this war that the British employed a new type of soldier. In European wars, the armies lined up and fought in the open. In North America, the Native Americans fought using other techniques like ambush and raids against civilians. During the French and Indian War, the British recruited a group of fighters in New England that were to function as scouts and as a countermeasure to the type of fighting done by the Native Americans.

Robert Rogers of New Hampshire had served as a scout in the previous war and was an able woodsman and fighter. Rogers was put in charge of a company of fighters called Rangers by the British. They were soon known as Rogers's Rangers and were involved in numerous scouting operations and battles. The Rangers dressed as woodsmen and were able to fight in the woods just like their Native American enemies. One of their well known battles was fought in spring 1758. The Rangers attacked a group of Native Americans not realizing that they were greatly outnumbered. They ended up losing the battle, but it was remarkable because it was fought on snowshoes.

In the early years of the French and Indian War, it seemed that the French had the upper hand. However, as Britain put more and more resources into the campaign in North America, the tide turned. Eventually, with the help of colonial militias and special forces like Rogers's Rangers, the British forces penetrated the very heart of New France along the St. Lawrence River. In 1759, as the British prepared to attack Quebec, Rogers's Rangers were given a special mission. The town of Saint Francis (50 miles downriver from Montreal, near modern-day Pierre Ville, Quebec) was home to a large number of Christian Native Americans. It was the

(continues)

Robert Rogers led a group that became known as Rogers's Rangers in the fight against the French and their Native American allies in the French and Indian War. *(National Archives of Canada)*

(continued)

base for many of the raids that were conducted against the frontiers of northern New England and New York. Rogers and 200 of his Rangers were sent to destroy the town.

Just before dawn on October 2, 1759, the Rangers attacked. The people of the town never stood a chance and were wiped out. It is reported that the Rangers found more than 600 English scalps hanging in the village. The people of New England were much more excited by the destruction of St. Francis than they were by the capture of Quebec the same day. In 1760, the British mounted their final campaign against the French at Montreal. The capture of Montreal brought the fighting to an end in North America, but it was 1763 before the final terms were agreed to in the Treaty of Paris.

Pierre and Miquelon remain French territory today. Britain now controlled the entire continent of North America east of the Mississippi, with the exception of New Orleans and a poorly defined stretch of land along the Gulf Coast referred to as northwest Florida, which belonged to the Spanish. These two exceptions and everything to the west of the Mississippi belonged to Spain, at least for a while.

Although no battles were fought in Connecticut during the French and Indian War, the impact on the colony was immense. Despite the profits made by merchants during the war, many in the colony had come to resent the presence of British troops in North America. Connecticut and the other colonies involved had not agreed to form a single colonial authority at the Albany Congress in 1754. However, there was a growing sentiment that the colonies could take care of themselves.

Ideas about the colonies were also changing in England. The French and Indian War had doubled the country's national debt, and many thought that it was time for the colonies to pay their share. Up until this point, the English kings and their advisers had allowed the colonies to operate with little interference from London. Only a few taxes were enacted, and many of those were not enforced. The result had been a huge growth in commerce between the colonies and Great Britain. Merchants on both sides of the Atlantic had become wealthy because of the freewheeling and often illegal trade in the colonies.

The attempts to enforce existing trade laws such as the Molasses Act of 1733, and the passing of numerous new laws and taxes contributed greatly to the independence movement in Connecticut. Many of the leaders of the independence movement came from the merchants and traders who were hit

Albany Plan
(1754)

When Connecticut and six other colonies sent representatives to Albany, New York, in 1754, one of their most pressing topics was defending the colonies against the French and their Native American allies. Governor William Shirley of Massachusetts and Benjamin Franklin of Pennsylvania worked together to come up with a plan of defense. What they suggested is known as the Albany Plan. It called for colonial defenses to be put under the control of one chief military executive and for there to be one commissioner for Indian affairs for all the colonies.

In addition, the plan had provisions for a grand council of delegates that would have representatives from all thirteen colonies. The Albany Plan was taken back to the seven colonies that had sent representatives. Not one colonial legislature agreed to the plan. In 1754, there was too much competition between the colonies for them to unite in their common defense. Over the next 20 years, that would change dramatically.

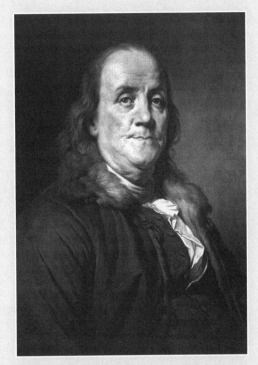

Benjamin Franklin, shown here, and Governor William Shirley proposed the Albany Plan as a way to defend the colonies against the French and their Native American allies. *(National Archives/DOD, War & Conflict, #65)*

hardest by Britain's attempts to collect what they thought they were owed.

After the Treaty of Paris, France continued to cause problems. The French encouraged trade with the English colonies although it was illegal in the eyes of the British. When the Revolution came, the French were eager to take the side of the colonies in retribution for their own losses in North America at the hands of the British.

7

Road to Revolution

THE SUGAR ACT,
April 5, 1764

The defeat of France in North America had cost a lot of money, and the English government had doubled its debt paying for the war. To help reduce the debt and pay for the cost of maintaining a standing army in North America, Parliament decided that the colonies should contribute. On April 5, 1764, Parliament passed what was known as the Sugar Act. This law was designed to reform some of the previous trade laws that had not worked and to raise revenue by taxing certain trade goods, including sugar and molasses.

In the past, many in the sugar trade had regularly avoided paying duties by trading with the French colonies in the Caribbean, even when France and England were at war. Many people in coastal Connecticut were dependent on the sugar trade and the distilleries that made rum for their livelihood. Those most affected by the Sugar Act were very upset. However, the Sugar Act did not affect that many people and failed to generate the income that Parliament had expected. When they tried to come up with another tax, Parliament set off a protest movement in Connecticut and the other colonies that would lead to the American Revolution.

THE STAMP ACT,
March 22, 1765

Parliament passed its next tax on the colonies on March 22, 1765, and it was called the Stamp Act. This law, which was scheduled to go into effect on November 1, 1765, set off a series of protests in the colonies that increased the widening gap between the colonies and the government in London. The Stamp Act was not a new idea. Stamp taxes were a way of raising revenue that had been used in England and even by some of the colonial governments. Under the Stamp Act, all legal and business documents, newspapers, licenses, and a few consumer products like dice and playing cards needed to have a tax stamp on them before they could be sold or processed.

In Connecticut, there were two major objections to the Stamp Act. First, the Connecticut charter gave the colony more self-government than other colonies. Because of this, leaders asserted Parliament did not have the right to pass laws for them. Also, throughout the colonies people were upset because they had no voice in the government in England, which was now trying to tax them. Among those who would soon be referred to as "Patriots," "No taxation without representation" became the slogan that brought them together.

People in Connecticut became some of the leaders in the protest movement that erupted after the passage of the Stamp Act. Jonathan Trumbull, who would be governor during the Revolution, and Israel Putnam, the Connecticut hero of the French and Indian War, got together with a number of other Patriots in Connecticut and formed a group known as the Sons of Liberty. This group led most of the protests against English authority in the colony. Rhode Island and Massachusetts soon followed Connecticut's lead and formed their own branches of the Sons of Liberty. The idea then spread throughout the colonies.

When affixed to goods, this stamp signified that a tax had been paid upon purchase. Many colonists felt that the British unfairly introduced these taxes when they implemented the Stamp Act in 1765, which affected goods ranging from business transactions to playing cards. *(Library of Congress, Prints and Photographs Division [LC-USZ61-539])*

Colonists denounce the Stamp Act in 1765. *(Library of Congress)*

Jared Ingersoll, a New Haven lawyer, was appointed to serve as the stamp agent in Connecticut. Ingersoll became the focus of much of the protest against the Stamp Act in Connecticut. In New Haven, Lebanon, Norwich, and other Connecticut towns, protests were held. In some cases, the protesters just asked for Ingersoll's resignation. In others, dummies, or effigies, that represented Ingersoll were made and mock trials held. After "conviction" by the protesters, his dummy was hung and/or burned.

In September, Ingersoll headed to Hartford to talk to Governor Thomas Fitch, who thought the people of Connecticut should obey the law. Ingersoll hoped the governor would help him put the Stamp Act into effect. As Ingersoll rode toward Hartford, he began to attract a large group of protesters. By the time he reached Wethersfield, there were more than 500 people waiting for him. The Sons of Liberty threatened Ingersoll with clubs and forced him to resign in front of the crowd. After resigning, he was allowed to continue on to Hartford. By the time he

Sons of Liberty

When the Stamp Act was passed by Parliament in 1765, people in Connecticut formed the first group in the colonies to protest it. One of the few opponents of the Stamp Act in Parliament's House of Commons, Isaac Barré, called the protesters the "sons of liberty." The Patriot leaders in Connecticut adopted the name, and there were soon groups calling themselves the Sons of Liberty throughout the colonies. It was the Sons of Liberty who organized protests to the Stamp Act in Connecticut. Similar groups in the other colonies would later hold "tea parties" in Boston, New Jersey, and South Carolina when the Tea Act was passed.

Israel Putnam, shown in this engraving, and Jonathan Trumbull formed the Sons of Liberty in response to the passage of the Stamp Act. *(National Archives of Canada)*

reached the governor, there were more than 1,000 people in the mob. In front of the General Assembly building, Ingersoll resigned again.

Similar protests took place throughout the colonies. In some places like Boston, the houses of stamp agents and other government officials were destroyed by angry mobs. When November 1, 1765, arrived, no one in any of the colonies, except Georgia, dared issue any stamps. In March 1766, Parliament repealed the Stamp Act, and many in the colonies thought that would be the end of it. However, accompanying the repeal of the Stamp Act was a bill called the Declaratory Act. This stated that Parliament had the right to pass any laws they saw fit to regulate the English colonies.

THE TOWNSHEND DUTIES,
June 29, 1767

Had Parliament worked with the colonies, some historians believe that they probably could have resolved many of their differences and the thirteen colonies would have remained part of the British Empire. However, the king and others in the government thought the people in the colonies were behaving like naughty children and should be taught a lesson. They failed to realize that by this time many in the colonies felt little allegiance to England and the king. They had been born in the colonies and considered themselves Americans first. Many others had arrived in the American colonies from Ireland, Scotland, and other countries in Europe, and they also felt little or no allegiance to England.

In 1767, Parliament decided to try again and tax the colonies. One of the objections to the Stamp Act was that it was a direct tax on the people of the colonies who were not represented in Parliament. This time they chose to enact a series of duties on trade goods such as glass, lead, colorings for paint, paper, and tea. These taxes would be paid by merchants and would therefore be an indirect tax.

At first, people in the colonies were unsure how to react to the Townshend Duties. As time went on, though, the more radical leaders among the Patriots once again moved people to take action. Many merchants agreed to not import any of the goods included in the Townshend Duties. Many colonists agreed and found alternatives to drinking tea, which was a popular beverage in the colonies. By 1770, tensions between British officials and soldiers in the colonies and the Patriots had reached the boiling point. On January 18, 1770, in New York City, where off-duty British soldiers worked as day laborers and were taking jobs away from colonists, a riot broke out that is known as the Battle of Golden Hill. This was in reality a brawl between soldiers and a mob, and although many were injured, none were killed. This was not the case on March 5, 1770, when an angry mob of protesters outside the customhouse in Boston threw chunks of ice and snowballs at the British soldiers guarding the building.

It has never been learned who gave the order, but the soldiers raised their rifles to apparently frighten the mob. When this had no effect, someone yelled fire, and the soldiers fired into the crowd, killing five of the Patriots. This event is known as the Boston Massacre. The Townshend Duties turned out to be another failure for Parliament, and all of them except the duty on tea were repealed in April 1770. At this point, although some had died in the name of liberty, very few in the colonies were thinking about revolution and independence. In fact, after the repeal of the Townshend Acts it was relatively quiet throughout the colonies. But that would not last.

THE TEA ACT,
May 10, 1773

Three years after the Boston Massacre, Parliament once again meddled in the commerce of the English colonies. The British East India Company, which many government officials had invested in, was in trouble financially and in danger of bankruptcy. Under the existing rules, the East India Company had a monopoly on the tea trade with the British colonies in Asia. However, all their tea had to be shipped to England, where it was sold to a number of different wholesalers who paid a tax and then marked up the tea and sold it.

Some of this tea was exported to America, where another tax was applied and the price was again raised. This made English tea

To protest the passage of the Tea Act, some male colonists, disguised as American Indians, boarded three ships in Boston Harbor on December 16, 1773, and dumped hundreds of cases of tea into the harbor. The event became known as the Boston Tea Party. *(Library of Congress)*

very expensive, so many people in the colonies drank tea that was smuggled into the colonies from the Dutch. The Tea Act made it possible for the East India Company to sell tea directly to the colonies, which actually made the tea cheaper, but it gave the company a monopoly on tea sales in America. When the first shipment of tea arrived in Boston on December 16, 1773, members of the Massachusetts Sons of Liberty disguised as Indians boarded the ship and dumped £10,000 worth of tea in Boston Harbor.

The Boston Tea Party set off a whole new set of protests in the colonies. It also angered the king and Parliament, which quickly passed a number of laws that were intended to teach the colonies a lesson. Instead, they led directly to fighting between British soldiers and colonial militia known as "minutemen" because they trained to be ready to fight at a minute's notice.

THE INTOLERABLE ACTS, 1774

While people in the colonies celebrated the defiance of the Tea Act at the Boston Tea Party, Parliament passed a series of laws that they called the Coercive Acts that were intended to make an example of the people of Boston and Massachusetts. The colonists in America referred to the new laws as the Intolerable Acts.

The first law was called the Boston Port Bill (March 31, 1774). It closed the port of Boston until the tea that had been dumped into the harbor was paid for. Instead of getting the people in Boston to pay up, the bill united Patriots throughout the colonies. As food and other necessities became scarce in Boston, other colonies sent relief supplies that were landed in ports that were not closed, such as those in Connecticut, and then transported overland to Boston.

The second Intolerable Act was known as the Massachusetts Government Act (May 20, 1774). This law took power away from the government of Massachusetts and transferred it to Crown officials in the colony. This act worried many people who had previously thought that the existing forms of government were protected by colonial charters and previous Crown rulings. Realizing that the Crown could arbitrarily change local government in the colonies brought many new people to the Patriot cause.

The other three parts of the Intolerable Acts also upset people in America. The Administration of Justice Act (May 20, 1774) allowed the Crown to transfer court cases to any court they chose. Someone committing a crime in Boston could even be taken to London for trial. The Quartering Act (June 2, 1774) made it the responsibility of the colonies to support British troops stationed in the colonies. The final part of the acts was the Quebec Act (June 22, 1774). It gave special privileges to the primarily French/Catholic people of Canada. It also included a restriction on the westward expansion of the thirteen colonies by making the lands west of the Appalachians part of Canada.

Although the first two Intolerable Acts created the most controversy, all five contributed to the growing feeling that the colonies and the Crown might not be able to easily solve their problems. However, many people wanted to try, and it was agreed that all the colonies would send representatives to a meeting, known as the First Continental Congress, in Philadelphia in September 1774.

Silas Deane represented Connecticut at the First Continental Congress. *(Library of Congress, Prints and Photographs Division [LC-USZ62-26779])*

THE FIRST CONTINENTAL CONGRESS, September 5 to October 26, 1774

When the call went out for a congress of delegates from the thirteen colonies to gather in Philadelphia in September 1774, the leaders of Connecticut selected three representatives—Roger Sherman, Silas Deane, and Eliphalet Dyer, who had been one of the founders of the Sons of Liberty—to represent Connecticut. Most of the delegates hoped that there could be a peaceful settlement of differences between the British government and the 13 American colonies. They called for all the colonies to stop using goods that were imported from England. If that boycott did not work, the First Continental Congress delegates decided they would then ask people to stop selling goods produced in the colonies to England.

Although the hope of the delegates was to avoid a fight with the Crown, they suggested that all the colonies start organizing and drilling militia in case war broke out. In Connecticut, in October 1774, the General Assembly ordered the state's militia to start training. The assembly also instructed towns to start stockpiling ammunition and weapons that might be needed. The delegates of the First Continental Congress agreed to hold a second congress in 1775 to reassess the situation and see if other action was needed. Before they could meet for the Second Continental Congress, however, fighting broke out in Massachusetts and the American Revolution began.

8

War for Independence

LEXINGTON, CONCORD, AND BUNKER HILL, 1775

As militia groups throughout the colonies organized and began drilling in anticipation of war, tensions rose between the British soldiers stationed in Boston and the Patriot leaders of Massachusetts. On April 18, 1775, British troops marched out of Boston and headed for Lexington and Concord in the hopes of catching some of the Patriot leaders who had already left the area. The next morning, April 19, 1775, when the British reached Lexington Green, they were met by a small force of local militia. When ordered to lay down their weapons by the much larger British force, the Patriots broke ranks and tried to escape. The British soldiers opened fire and killed eight colonists and wounded 10 others.

When word spread of the shooting in Lexington, militias from all over the area were mobilized. By the time the British reached Concord, they were met by a much larger colonial force. A pitched battle was fought at the North Bridge in Concord, and then it was the British soldiers' turn to try to escape. As they retreated to Boston, they were harassed by militia sharpshooters who fired at them from the cover of the woods or the protection of stone walls. The British soldiers suffered 300 dead or wounded, while the Americans lost about 100 fighters. The American Revolution was now a reality.

The colonists and the British fought fiercely at North Bridge in Concord, Massachusetts, as seen in this 1859 engraving. *(National Archives/DOD, War & Conflict, #11)*

By April 20, 1775, the news of the Battle of Lexington and Concord had spread to Connecticut and throughout New England. It was soon news in all the colonies. The hopes of reconciliation with the Crown and Parliament had vanished in the clouds of smoke issued from the guns of dissent. Connecticut militia units headed for Boston with the hopes of driving the British into the harbor.

For the next two months, there were no major conflicts between the colonial militias that had gathered around Boston and the British forces that were trapped there. The militia leaders knew they needed to command the high ground around Boston and its harbor if they were going to drive out the British. Plans were made to fortify Dorchester Heights to the south of the city and Breed's and Bunker Hills that overlook the harbor from Charlestown to the north. During the night of June 16, 1775, about 1,000 colonial militia went to the top of Breed's and Bunker Hills. Approximately 200 militiamen from Connecticut were led by Israel Putnam. It was decided that they would dig in on Breed's Hill, which was not quite as tall as Bunker Hill but was closer to the harbor.

When the British soldiers in Boston woke up on June 17, 1775, they were greeted by the sight of the colonial force looking down their rifles at them. The British response was immediate. Warships were brought in to bombard Breed's Hill. Then a force of 2,000 redcoats, as the British soldiers were called, was sent to show the colonials what it was like to face an assault by troops from the greatest army in the world at the time.

Israel Putnam
(1718–1790)

Israel Putnam was born in Salem Village, Massachusetts (present-day Danvers), in 1718. In 1739, when he was 21, he married Hannah Pope, and the newlyweds moved to what is now Brooklyn, Connecticut. In Connecticut, the Putnams carved a successful farm out of the wilderness. They raised a large family with eight children. Two other children were born to the Putnams but did not survive their early childhoods. The Putnam farm was a model of success, with large orchards that included a variety of apples that Israel is credited with developing. They also had large flocks of sheep.

In 1755, Israel Putnam joined the Connecticut militia that was getting ready to fight in the French and Indian War. Putnam quickly rose through the ranks as he repeatedly showed his bravery and leadership in the raids he participated in against the French and their Indian allies in New York and Canada. At the time of the Stamp Act protests, Putnam was one of the first members of the Sons of Liberty in Connecticut.

When news of the Battle of Lexington and Concord reached Connecticut, it is reported that Israel Putnam left his plow in the middle of a field he was plowing and rode off to Boston. He covered the 70-mile distance in one day. Putnam was followed by 3,600 militiamen from Connecticut. When the Continental Congress sent George Washington to Boston as commander of the Continental army, he selected Putnam to be one of his generals. However, Putnam was not as good at leading large forces as he had been in leading small groups against the French. By 1776, Putnam was ill and in 1779 he had a stroke that ended his military career. He died in 1790 at the age of 72.

General Thomas Gage, the British commander, blundered when he instructed General Sir William Howe to lead his forces in a direct frontal assault. The British learned a hard lesson on the slopes of Breed's Hill. Instead of panicking in the face of 2,000 British soldiers marching up the hill in formation, Colonel William Prescott, the Patriot commander, had his troops hold their fire until the British were almost upon them. When the order to fire was given, the colonial marksmen mowed down the British soldiers and sent them retreating down the hill.

Once out of range, the British reset their formations and marched into the colonial sights again. The results were the same: the British suffered even more casualties and were sent back down

Israel Putnam is said to have left his plow in the middle of his field as he hurried to help defend the colonies against the British forces. *(National Archives/DOD, War & Conflict, #13)*

"Whites of Their Eyes"

"Don't one of you fire until you see the whites of their eyes," Colonel William Prescott is reported to have said to his men as the British troops marched up Breed's Hill. Other accounts give Israel Putnam of Connecticut credit for making this famous statement.

again. On the third assault, the British finally captured Breed's Hill when the colonials ran out of gunpowder, but British losses were so heavy that they were unable to pursue the American fighters. Records show that 226 British soldiers died and 828 were wounded in capturing Breed's Hill. On the colonial side, 140 were killed and 271 were wounded.

The American Revolution was just starting and the Battle of Bunker Hill, as it was called, was not a significant victory in terms of territory won and lost. However, in the psychological battle between the mighty British army and the untrained and undisciplined American forces, the impact of the battle was immense. From this battle forward, the British proceeded with much greater respect for their adversaries and a sense of caution. Although the colonials lost the hill, they gained a huge boost of confidence. They may not have had fancy red uniforms, but the minutemen of Connecticut and other colonies that held in the face of the attacks on Breed's Hill proved they were a match for the British regulars.

General Gage had now commanded two attacks against the colonial forces. At both Lexington and Concord, and at Breed's Hill, his forces had been outdone by the colonials. When word of the casualties sustained at Breed's Hill reached London, Gage was recalled. General Howe took over as commander of the British forces in North America. Some have argued that it was Howe's cautious attitude, after leading the attack on Breed's Hill, that may have been the ultimate key to an American victory in the War for Independence.

DECLARING INDEPENDENCE

The Second Continental Congress met in Philadelphia on May 10, 1775. Connecticut sent Roger Sherman to again represent the colony. Sherman had three new delegates to accompany him: Sam Huntington, Oliver Wolcott, and William Williams. At first, the congress wanted to take a defensive posture rather than further provoke the British forces in North America. However, in May 1775, two Connecticut natives, Ethan Allen from Litchfield and Benedict Arnold from New Haven, led a force to Lake Champlain where they captured Fort Ticonderoga from the British. The cannons from Ticonderoga were hauled over the snow to Boston,

This engraving dramatizes Ethan Allen's and Benedict Arnold's capture of Fort Ticonderoga in New York.
(Library of Congress, Prints and Photographs Division [LC-USZ62-96539])

IN CONGRESS, JULY 4, 1776.

A DECLARATION

BY THE REPRESENTATIVES OF THE

UNITED STATES OF AMERICA,

IN GENERAL CONGRESS ASSEMBLED.

WHEN in the Course of human Events, it becomes neceſſary for one People to diſſolve the Political Bands which have connected them with another, and to aſſume among the Powers of the Earth, the ſeparate and equal Station to which the Laws of Nature and of Nature's God entitle them, a decent Reſpect to the Opinions of Mankind requires that they ſhould declare the cauſes which impel them to the Separation.

We hold theſe Truths to be ſelf-evident, that all Men are created equal, that they are endowed by their Creator with certain unalienable Rights, that among theſe are Life, Liberty, and the Purſuit of Happineſs--That to ſecure theſe Rights, Governments are inſtituted among Men, deriving their juſt Powers from the Conſent of the Governed, that whenever any Form of Government becomes deſtructive of theſe Ends, it is the Right of the People to alter or to aboliſh it, and to inſtitute new Government, laying its Foundation on ſuch Principles, and organizing its Powers in ſuch Form, as to them ſhall ſeem moſt likely to effect their Safety and Happineſs. Prudence, indeed, will dictate that Governments long eſtabliſhed ſhould not be changed for light and tranſient Cauſes; and accordingly all Experience hath ſhewn, that Mankind are more diſpoſed to ſuffer, while Evils are ſufferable, than to right themſelves by aboliſhing the Forms to which they are accuſtomed. But when a long Train of Abuſes and Uſurpations, purſuing invariably the ſame Object, evinces a Deſign to reduce them under abſolute Deſpotiſm, it is their Right, it is their Duty, to throw off ſuch Government, and to provide new Guards for their future Security. Such has been the patient Sufferance of theſe Colonies; and ſuch is now the Neceſſity which conſtrains them to alter their former Syſtems of Government. The Hiſtory of the preſent King of Great-Britain is a Hiſtory of repeated Injuries and Uſurpations, all having in direct Object the Eſtabliſhment of an abſolute Tyranny over theſe States. To prove this, let Facts be ſubmitted to a candid World.

He has refuſed his Aſſent to Laws, the moſt wholeſome and neceſſary for the public Good.

He has forbidden his Governors to paſs Laws of immediate and preſſing Importance, unleſs ſuſpended in their Operation till his Aſſent ſhould be obtained; and when ſo ſuſpended, he has utterly neglected to attend to them.

He has refuſed to paſs other Laws for the Accommodation of large Diſtricts of People, unleſs thoſe People would relinquiſh the Right of Repreſentation in the Legiſlature, a Right ineſtimable to them, and formidable to Tyrants only.

He has called together Legiſlative Bodies at Places unuſual, uncomfortable, and diſtant from the Depoſitory of their public Records, for the ſole Purpoſe of fatiguing them into Compliance with his Meaſures.

He has diſſolved Repreſentative Houſes repeatedly, for oppoſing with manly Firmneſs his Invaſions on the Rights of the People.

He has refuſed for a long Time, after ſuch Diſſolutions, to cauſe others to be elected; whereby the Legiſlative Powers, incapable of Annihilation, have returned to the People at large for their exerciſe; the State remaining in the mean time expoſed to all the Dangers of Invaſion from without, and Convulſions within.

He has endeavoured to prevent the Population of theſe States; for that Purpoſe obſtructing the Laws for Naturalization of Foreigners; refuſing to paſs others to encourage their Migrations hither, and raiſing the Conditions of new Appropriations of Lands.

He has obſtructed the Adminiſtration of Juſtice, by refuſing his Aſſent to Laws for eſtabliſhing Judiciary Powers.

He has made Judges dependent on his Will alone, for the Tenure of their Offices, and the Amount and Payment of their Salaries.

He has erected a Multitude of new Offices, and ſent hither Swarms of Officers to harraſs our People, and eat out their Subſtance.

He has kept among us, in Times of Peace, Standing Armies, without the conſent of our Legiſlatures.

He has affected to render the Military independent of and ſuperior to the Civil Power.

He has combined with others to ſubject us to a Juriſdiction foreign to our Conſtitution, and unacknowledged by our Laws; giving his Aſſent to their Acts of pretended Legiſlation:

For quartering large Bodies of Armed Troops among us:

For protecting them, by a mock Trial, from Puniſhment for any Murders which they ſhould commit on the Inhabitants of theſe States:

For cutting off our Trade with all Parts of the World:

For impoſing Taxes on us without our Conſent:

For depriving us, in many Caſes, of the Benefits of Trial by Jury:

For tranſporting us beyond Seas to be tried for pretended Offences:

For aboliſhing the free Syſtem of Engliſh Laws in a neighbouring Province, eſtabliſhing therein an arbitrary Government, and enlarging its Boundaries, ſo as to render it at once an Example and fit Inſtrument for introducing the ſame abſolute Rule into theſe Colonies:

For taking away our Charters, aboliſhing our moſt valuable Laws, and altering fundamentally the Forms of our Governments:

For ſuſpending our own Legiſlatures, and declaring themſelves inveſted with Power to legiſlate for us in all Caſes whatſoever.

He has abdicated Government here, by declaring us out of his Protection and waging War againſt us.

He has plundered our Seas, ravaged our Coaſts, burnt our Towns, and deſtroyed the Lives of our People.

He is, at this Time, tranſporting large Armies of foreign Mercenaries to compleat the Works of Death, Deſolation, and Tyranny, already begun with circumſtances of Cruelty and Perfidy, ſcarcely paralleled in the moſt barbarous Ages, and totally unworthy the Head of a civilized Nation.

He has conſtrained our fellow Citizens taken Captive on the high Seas to bear Arms againſt their Country, to become the Executioners of their Friends and Brethren, or to fall themſelves by their Hands.

He has excited domeſtic Inſurrections amongſt us, and has endeavoured to bring on the Inhabitants of our Frontiers, the mercileſs Indian Savages, whoſe known Rule of Warfare, is an undiſtinguiſhed Deſtruction, of all Ages, Sexes and Conditions.

In every ſtage of theſe Oppreſſions we have Petitioned for Redreſs in the moſt humble Terms: Our repeated Petitions have been anſwered only by repeated Injury. A Prince, whoſe Character is thus marked by every act which may define a Tyrant, is unfit to be the Ruler of a free People.

Nor have we been wanting in Attentions to our Britiſh Brethren. We have warned them from Time to Time of Attempts by their Legiſlature to extend an unwarrantable Juriſdiction over us. We have reminded them of the Circumſtances of our Emigration and Settlement here. We have appealed to their native Juſtice and Magnanimity, and we have conjured them by the Ties of our common Kindred to diſavow theſe Uſurpations, which, would inevitably interrupt our Connections and Correſpondence. They too have been deaf to the Voice of Juſtice and of Conſanguinity. We muſt, therefore, acquieſce in the Neceſſity, which denounces our Separation, and hold them, as we hold the reſt of Mankind, Enemies in War, in Peace, Friends.

We, therefore, the Repreſentatives of the UNITED STATES OF AMERICA, in GENERAL CONGRESS, Aſſembled, appealing to the Supreme Judge of the World for the Rectitude of our Intentions, do, in the Name, and by Authority of the good People of theſe Colonies, ſolemnly Publiſh and Declare, That theſe United Colonies are, and of Right ought to be, FREE AND INDEPENDENT STATES; that they are abſolved from all Allegiance to the Britiſh Crown, and that all political Connection between them and the State of Great-Britain, is and ought to be totally diſſolved; and that as FREE AND INDEPENDENT STATES, they have full Power to levy War, conclude Peace, contract Alliances, eſtabliſh Commerce, and to do all other Acts and Things which INDEPENDENT STATES may of right do. And for the ſupport of this Declaration, with a firm Reliance on the Protection of divine Providence, we mutually pledge to each other our Lives, our Fortunes, and our ſacred Honor.

Signed by ORDER and in BEHALF of the CONGRESS,

JOHN HANCOCK, PRESIDENT.

ATTEST.
CHARLES THOMSON, SECRETARY.

PHILADELPHIA: PRINTED BY JOHN DUNLAP.

One of the first and boldest acts of the Second Continental Congress was to compose and sign the Declaration of Independence in summer 1776. *(National Archives, Old Military and Civil Records, NWCTB-360-ITEM1-ITEM1VOL3P94)*

The First Paragraph of the Declaration of Independence

Thomas Jefferson of Virginia is given credit for writing the Declaration of Independence although he was assisted by a committee that included Connecticut delegate Roger Sherman. It begins with the following paragraph:

When in the Course of human events, it becomes necessary for one people to dissolve the political bands which have connected them with another, and to assume among the Powers of the earth, the separate and equal station to which the Laws of Nature and of Nature's God entitle them, a decent respect to the opinions of mankind requires that they should declare the causes which impel them to the separation.

where George Washington was able to drive out the British in March 1776.

As summer 1776 approached, it was clear that neither side, the British nor the Patriots in the colonies, were going to give in easily. The delegates to the Second Continental Congress, which stayed in session throughout the seven years of the war, decided it was time to talk about independence. A committee of five delegates was appointed to draw up a document stating the colonial position. Although Thomas Jefferson is given most of the credit for writing what would become the Declaration of Independence, he was assisted by the other members of his committee, which included Benjamin Franklin, John Adams, Robert R. Livingston, and Connecticut delegate Roger Sherman.

On July 2, 1776, 12 of the 13 delegations voted in favor of independence. New York did not vote on that day but made it unanimous two days later. On July 4, 1776, the Second Continental Congress adopted the Declaration of Independence written by Thomas Jefferson and his committee, and the United States was born.

Declaring independence was easier than achieving it. The American Revolution, which had begun in April 1775, did not end until the Battle of Yorktown in 1781. Although no major battles were fought in Connecticut, the state played a major role in winning the war.

CONNECTICUT IN THE REVOLUTION

The American Revolution started in Massachusetts and then bypassed Connecticut to continue in New York, New Jersey, Pennsylvania, and the South. As George Washington led the Continental army in the war, he was well supported by Connecticut. Between 30,000 and 40,000 Connecticut soldiers fought in the Continental army. Only Massachusetts contributed more soldiers to the war. One of Connecticut's most famous soldiers was Nathan Hale, who was captured and executed by the British in New York City for being a spy.

In addition, Connecticut supplied many of the materials for Washington's army. Many people in the Connecticut River valley, which had already become a manufacturing center, turned much of their energy toward supplying the war effort. The first gunpowder mill in North America was started at Hartford in

On October 11, 1776, Benedict Arnold commanded a small fleet of ships on Lake Champlain against the British forces in the Battle of Valcour Island. Although the colonial fleet lost the battle, they prevented the British from invading farther into the United States and possibly attacking Fort Ticonderoga. This illustration depicts the colonial ships ready for battle. *(National Archives of Canada)*

Loyalists and Patriots

Benedict Arnold is the most famous colonial to have fought with the British because he started out as a Patriot soldier and then betrayed his own forces. Throughout the colonies, many people remained loyal to the British king. These people were called Loyalists, and at the beginning of the war one-third of the people in the colonies considered themselves Loyalists. At the same time, another third of the population considered themselves Patriots who wanted to break away from British rule. The other third was neutral.

Connecticut did not fit the profile when it came to Patriots and Loyalists. In Connecticut, it is estimated only about 6 percent of the population were Loyalists and most of them lived in the southwest corner of the state. This gave Connecticut a much higher percentage of Patriots than any of the other thirteen original colonies.

1775. Other factories produced rifles, cannons, uniforms, blankets, and other goods needed for the war. The farms of Connecticut supplied desperately needed food for the amy. In winter 1778, when Washington's army was suffering through the exceptionally cold and snowy winter at Valley Forge, Pennsylvania, it was cattle from Connecticut, sent by Governor Jonathan Trumbull, that helped prevent an even worse disaster for the soldiers.

A large portion of the supplies that passed through Connecticut to the Continental army were captured from British supply ships. The government of Connecticut commissioned a few naval ships and also issued over 200 letters of marque to private ships, giving them authority to attack British shipping. These ships were known as privateers and

Nathan Hale
(1755–1776)

Nathan Hale was born in Coventry, Connecticut, on June 6, 1755, and was one of 12 children. His parents hoped he would be a minister, but Hale chose to be a teacher after graduating from Yale when he was 18. He taught in East Haddam and New London before joining the Continental army in 1775. After fighting in the siege of Boston, he was promoted to captain. Captain Hale proved himself an able leader in the Battle of Long Island (New York). He was the only one to volunteer when George Washington asked for someone to go into New York City and gather information about the British force there.

Hale snuck into the city by posing as a Dutch schoolteacher and gathered information that would have been helpful to Washington and the Patriot forces. However, as Hale tried to leave the city, he was captured by British troops. Some have suggested that Hale was betrayed by a cousin of his who had remained loyal to the British. On September 21, 1776, Hale was sentenced to be executed as a spy without being given a trial. Just before he was hanged on September 22, 1776, Hale is reported to have made the statement

This statue honors Nathan Hale, a spy captured and hanged by the British during the Revolutionary War. *(Library of Congress, Prints and Photographs Division [LC-USZ6-195])*

that has made him one of America's greatest heroes, "I only regret that I have but one life to lose for my country."

were responsible for capturing around 500 British ships during the war.

When a ship was captured, it was sent into one of Connecticut's many ports, where its goods were sold and the profits split among the owner and crew. The warehouses of Connecticut were stuffed with seized British supplies, which were then passed to the Patriot forces. In part because of the success of Connecticut's privateers, the British conducted a number of raids against Connecticut. The first took place in April 1777, when a British force attacked Danbury in western Connecticut. During the raid, the British burned warehouses that were full of supplies that were to be sent to Washington and his army.

In February 1779, a British raid on Greenwich failed when General Israel Putnam arrived with a large force and chased the British back to New York. The other two raids on Connecticut were even more costly. On July 5, 1779, British troops attacked New Haven, which was a shipbuilding center. Part of the town was destroyed and

George Washington and his troops spent the winter of 1777–78 at Valley Forge, Pennsylvania, about 20 miles from Philadelphia, which was occupied by the British. The colonial forces had little food or supplies at their winter camp. Governor Jonathan Trumbull sent cattle from Connecticut to help sustain the soldiers. *(National Archives/DOD, War & Conflict, #36)*

Benedict Arnold served in the Continental army until his identity as a spy for the British was revealed. *(National Archives/DOD, War & Conflict, #62)*

a few people were killed and wounded. After the British left New Haven, they burned more than 200 buildings, half of which were homes, in Fairfield and then destroyed most of Norwalk.

The worst raid came just before the war ended. On September 6, 1781, Benedict Arnold, who had turned traitor and joined the British, led 2,000 troops to the mouth of the Thames River where

New London and Groton served as a staging area and storage depot for many of Connecticut's privateers.

Arnold took half the force and attacked New London. His men burned ships in the harbor, the wharves, and most of the buildings in the town. Across the river in Groton, Colonel William Ledyard and 150 Connecticut militia held Fort Griswold. Ledyard found himself surrounded by 1,000 British troops but refused to surrender. After holding the fort through a number of assaults, the colonial force was overwhelmed by the far larger British contingent. When the British soldiers burst through the fort's main gate, Ledyard knew the battle was over and tried to surrender. Instead, when he gave his sword to a British soldier, Ledyard was murdered with his own sword. The British went on to massacre more than 80 of the remaining soldiers.

Toward the end of the war, the French joined the Patriot cause against the British. They supplied both land and naval forces to help Washington's Continental army. On October 19, 1781, at Yorktown, Virginia, the British general Lord Cornwallis surrendered to George Washington and a combined force of French and Continental soldiers. There were Connecticut soldiers in the ranks of the American army at Yorktown as there had been at every major battle of the war. With the war over, it was time for the thirteen colonies to start building a nation. It would be a difficult time for many in Connecticut and the 12 other former British colonies.

9

Building a Nation

During the war, many people in Connecticut prospered because they grew, manufactured, or captured supplies that were sold to the Continental army. Within a relatively short period of time after the war ended, Connecticut and most of the other former colonies experienced an economic depression. The Continental Congress and most of the states had borrowed heavily to finance the war effort. Paper money issued by both the states and the Continental Congress had lost much of its value. After the war, it took £40 of Continental currency to buy £1 worth of goods. Many of the soldiers who had fought in the war were never paid or were paid with almost worthless paper money. Individual debt became a serious problem, especially since the vast majority of people in the colonies were farmers.

During the war, farm goods had brought high prices because large amounts of food had been needed to support the army. When all the soldiers returned home after the war, farm production increased, but the demand for surplus farm produce dropped. In western Massachusetts, an armed rebellion of farmers in jeopardy of losing their farms, led by Daniel Shays, threatened the stability of the state and required the militia to be called in.

In Connecticut, laws were passed to prevent creditors from throwing people off their farms. Governor Jonathan Trumbull and others in the state looked to the Continental Congress to

Jonathan Trumbull
(1710–1785)

Jonathan Trumbull was born in Lebanon, Connecticut in 1710. His father had a successful mercantile business, but his brother, Joseph, was expected to take over the business. Jonathan's parents hoped their younger son, would become a minister. Jonathan attended Harvard when he was 13 and graduated four years later. After serving as an apprentice with a local minister in Connecticut, he became a minister when he was 20. In 1732, his older brother Joseph was lost at sea along with the ship he was traveling on.

With his older brother gone, Jonathan Trumbull gave up the ministry and took over the family business. He exported meat and other food from Connecticut and ran a successful store in Lebanon. He entered politics in 1733 when he was elected to the colonial assembly. Over the following years, Trumbull held a number of positions in Connecticut's government, serving in the legislature, as a judge, as deputy governor, and as governor.

Jonathan Trumbull was the only colonial governor who remained in office before,

(continues)

Built in 1740, this house in Lebanon, Connecticut, belonged to Governor Jonathan Trumbull and was restored in 1935. *(Library of Congress, Prints and Photographs Division [HABS, CONN, 6-LEBA, 1-1])*

(continued)

during, and after the Revolution. He first became governor in 1769 and remained in office until he retired in 1784, a year after the Treaty of Paris officially ended the war between the former colonies and Great Britain. During the war, he helped the Patriot cause by securing needed supplies for the Continental army. George Washington was so appreciative of Trumbull's efforts on behalf of the Patriot cause that he referred to him as "Brother Jonathan." Trumbull died at his home in Lebanon in 1785.

help with the debt crisis. The federal government had no authority to keep an army or collect taxes. Without an army the federal government had not been able to assist in putting down Shays's Rebellion. Without the ability to create and collect taxes the government had no way of helping Connecticut or any of the other states with their financial crises. Much of the problem was caused by the weaknesses of the Articles of Confederation.

THE ARTICLES OF CONFEDERATION

The Second Continental Congress had proposed the Articles of Confederation in 1777. They were finally adopted by the states in 1781. Under the articles, there was a loose confederation of the states and a weak federal authority. Those who had proposed the articles did not want a strong central government. They wanted the bulk of the power to remain with the states. The experience of the tyrannical abuses of the British government in dealing with the colonies made many wary of giving much, if any, power to a central government.

During the war, the Continental Congress had acted on behalf of the country without any real official status. The Articles of Confederation were designed to formalize the union of the thirteen separate states. On paper, the articles seemed like a good compromise between those who wanted a strong federal government and those who did not.

However, when implemented, there were numerous problems. The biggest obstacle was that the federal government lacked a way to raise revenue other than asking the states for money. The federal

To all to whom these Presents shall come we the under signed Delegates of the States affixed to our Names send greeting. Whereas the Delegates of the United States of America in Congress assembled did on the fifteenth day of November in the Year of our Lord One Thousand Seven Hundred and Seventy seven and in the Second Year of the Independence of America agree to certain articles of Confederation and perpetual Union between the States of Newhampshire, Massachusetts-bay, Rhode-island and Providence Plantations, Connecticut, New York, New Jersey, Pennsylvania, Delaware, Maryland, Virginia, North Carolina, South Carolina and Georgia in the Words following, viz. "Articles of Confederation and perpetual Union between the states of Newhampshire, Massachusetts-bay, Rhodeisland and Providence Plantations, Connecticut, New-York, New-Jersey, Pennsylvania, Delaware, Maryland, Virginia, North-Carolina, South-Carolina and Georgia.

Article I. The Stile of this confederacy shall be "The United States of America."

Article II. Each state retains its sovereignty, freedom and independence, and every Power, Jurisdiction and right, which is not by this confederation expressly delegated to the United States, in Congress assembled.

Article III. The said states hereby severally enter into a firm league of friendship with each other, for their common defence, the security of their Liberties, and their mutual and general welfare, binding themselves to assist each other, against all force offered to, or attacks made upon them, or any of them, on account of religion, sovereignty, trade, or any other pretence whatever.

Article IV. The better to secure and perpetuate mutual friendship and intercourse among the people of the different states in this union, the free inhabitants of each of these states, paupers, vagabonds and fugitives from Justice excepted, shall be entitled to all privileges and immunities of free citizens in the several states; and the people of each state shall have free ingress and regress to and from any other state, and shall enjoy therein all the privileges of trade and commerce, subject to the same duties, impositions and restrictions as the inhabitants thereof respectively, provided that such restriction shall not extend so far as to prevent the removal of property imported into any state, to any other state of which the Owner is an inhabitant; provided also that no imposition, duties or restriction shall be laid by any state, on the property of the united states, or either of them.

If any Person guilty of, or charged with treason, felony, or other high misdemeanor in any state, shall flee from Justice, and be found in any of the united states, he shall upon demand of the Governor or executive power, of the state from which he fled, be delivered up and removed to the state having jurisdiction of his offence.

Full faith and credit shall be given in each of these states to the records, acts and judicial proceedings of the courts and magistrates of every other state.

Article V. For the more convenient management of the general

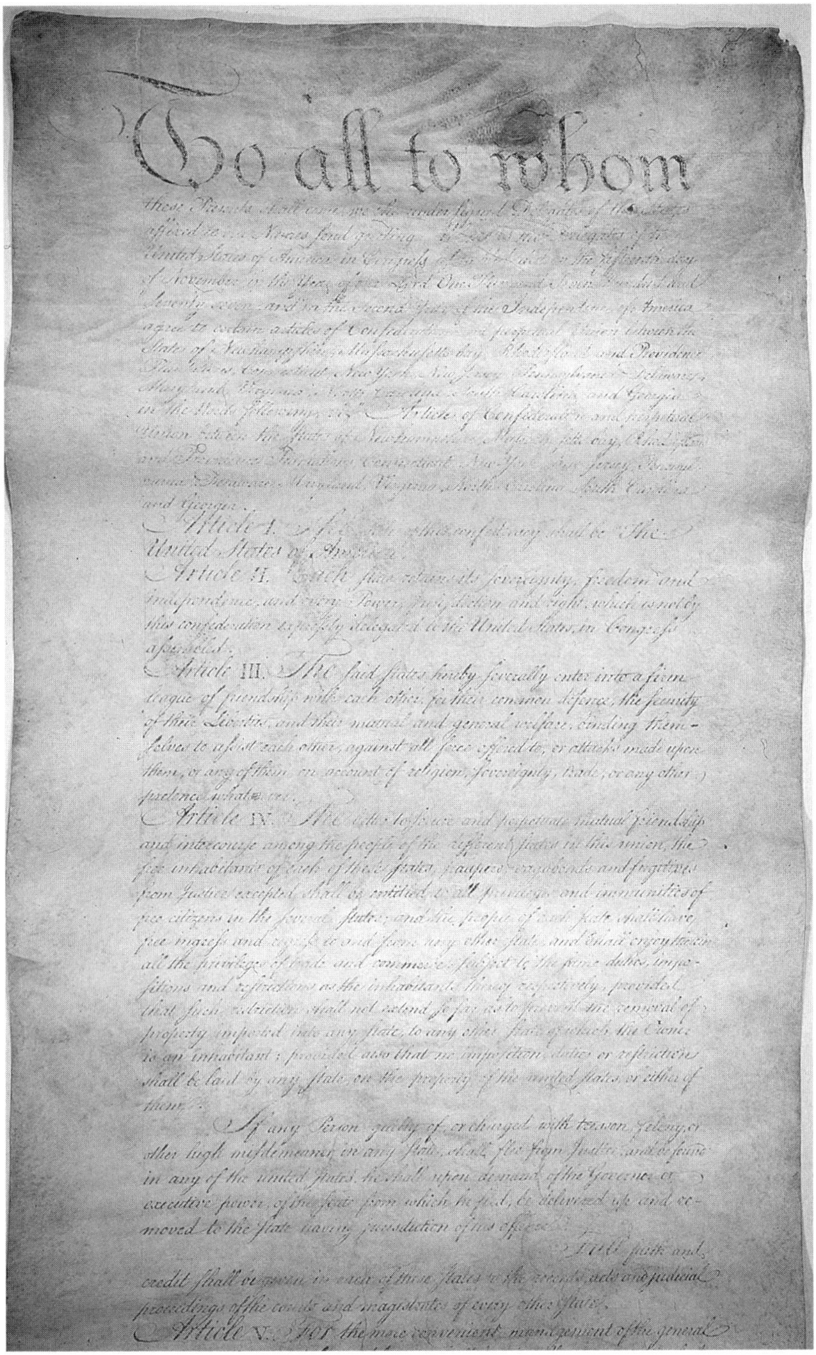

The Articles of Confederation, shown here, were written by a committee of the Continental Congress and intended as a constitution for the colonies. *(National Archives, National Archives Building, NWCTB-360-MISC-ROLL10F81)*

government also had no way to enforce its laws. In addition, the articles set up a difficult decision-making process. Each state, no matter its size, was given one vote. Often delegations could not come to a consensus on an issue and would not be able to cast a vote. This created another problem. The articles required all thirteen states to agree before any action could be taken by the federal government.

Under the Articles of Confederation, at times the thirteen states functioned independently of each other. Sometimes this put the states in opposition to each other in terms of trade and issues of boundaries. Shays's Rebellion and similar events in other colonies made it apparent to many that a stronger central government was needed. Those in favor of a stronger central government were known as Federalists. It was these people who lobbied for a convention to change the government by amending or replacing the Articles of Confederation.

THE CONSTITUTIONAL CONVENTION, 1787

At first, Connecticut had been happy to be a "free agent." Its interests in overseas trade, its prosperous farmers, and growing population made it likely that Connecticut would prosper once the postwar depression passed. However, many in the state saw the potential for serious problems in the future if there was not a federal authority to deal with issues like currency and rebellion. When the call went out for a convention to be held in Philadelphia in May 1787, Connecticut agreed to send delegates. The Connecticut delegates were Oliver Ellsworth, William Samuel Johnson, and Roger Sherman. Sherman was, except for Benjamin Franklin, the oldest delegate at what would be known as the Constitutional Convention and had an immense impact on the framing of the Constitution.

At the Constitutional Convention, the delegates divided into two groups. The people who supported a strong central government were called Federalists. The others were called Anti-Federalists because they wanted decision making power to remain with the states. Federalist ideas won out during the Constitutional Convention. However, the delegates hit an impasse when it came to

Roger Sherman
(1721–1793)

There are four documents that are seen as critical to the formation of the United States: the Articles of Association (1774), the Declaration of Independence (1776), the Articles of Confederation (1781), and the Constitution of the United States (1787). Only one person signed all four documents and that was Roger Sherman of Connecticut. Sherman was a perfect example of how brains and hard work allowed people to become successful in colonial America.

Sherman was born in Newton, Massachusetts, in 1721 and learned to be a cobbler, or shoemaker, like his father. In 1733, Roger Sherman loaded his shoe-making tools into a backpack and walked the 150 miles to New Milford, Connecticut. After two years there, he was appointed to his first public service job as county surveyor. Sherman loved to read and study, and he soon became a lawyer. In the 1750s, he went into the mercantile business with his brother and served as a legislator, lawyer, and judge.

In 1761, he moved to New Haven where he continued in politics. He was considered a person with good sense who could listen to both sides before he made up his mind. Sherman was selected as a delegate to both the First and Second Continental Congress and to the Constitutional Convention. It was at the latter where he may have performed his greatest service to the fledgling United States. When the convention reached a deadlock over represen-

Roger Sherman represented Connecticut at the First and Second Continental Congress and the Constitutional Convention. *(North Wind Picture Archives)*

tation in the national legislature, it was Sherman who proposed the Great (or Connecticut) Compromise. He proposed a senate based on equal representation and a house of representatives based on the population of a state. Some believe Connecticut's nickname, the Constitution State, can be attributed to Sherman's role in framing the U.S. Constitution.

Oliver Ellsworth represented Connecticut at the Constitutional Convention. *(Independence National Historical Park)*

decide how the states would be represented in the national legislature.

Large states, led by Virginia, put forth the Virginia Plan, which called for a legislature based on population, which would give the big states more power than the small states. The small states wanted the New Jersey Plan (called that because it was proposed by the New Jersey delegates) that called for each state to have an equal number of representatives in the federal legislature. For a time, it looked like the Constitution might not happen because the two sides refused to compromise.

Roger Sherman came up with the Great Compromise—sometimes called the Connecticut Compromise after Sherman's home state. Sherman proposed a legislature with two houses. The Senate would have two senators from each state, giving the smaller states an equal say in the voting for new laws. The other legislative body would be the House of Representatives. The number of representatives would be based on population, with a national census to count the population conducted every 10 years to reapportion the representatives.

Preamble to the U.S. Constitution

We the People of the United States, in Order to form a more perfect Union, establish Justice, insure domestic Tranquility, provide for the common defence, promote the general Welfare, and secure the Blessings of Liberty to ourselves and our Posterity, do ordain and establish this Constitution for the United States of America.

On September 17, 1787, the Constitution was passed by the Constitutional Convention. Nine states had to ratify it before it became the governing document of the United States. *(National Archives)*

Connecticut politics were extremely divided on the eve of the U.S. Constitution's ratification in 1787. In this image, Connecticut is symbolized by the wagon sinking into the mud under all its debt and problems and being pulled on both sides by disagreeing leaders. *(Library of Congress, Prints and Photographs Division [LC-USZC4-1722])*

This type of legislature is called bicameral because it has two parts. Sherman's Great Compromise was accepted by the delegates to the Constitutional Convention and has worked well, continuing to balance the power to make laws more than 200 years after the Constitution was adopted.

Adoption of the Constitution was based on a set of rules created at the Constitutional Convention. It had been decided that the new constitution would go into effect when nine states had ratified it. As soon as the Constitution was passed by the convention the delegates from Delaware rushed home. Its state legislature was the first to approve the new constitution on December 7, 1787. In early January 1788, each town in Connecticut sent a representative to Hartford to discuss and vote on the Constitution. After much discussion the delegates voted 128 to 40 to accept the Constitution. This made Connecticut the fifth state to approve the new constitution. The Constitution went into effect on June 21, 1788, when the delegates in Concord, New Hampshire, voted 57 to 47 in favor of it, making New Hampshire the ninth state.

In the early days under the Constitution, Connecticut prospered. Manufacturing of textiles and a variety of other goods turned the state into an industrial giant as the 18th century ended. Some of the earliest insurance companies in the country also fueled the economy of the state. The people of Connecticut have remained proud of the part their ancestors played in creating the United States.

Connecticut Time Line

1614

★ Adriaen Block sails up the Connecticut River.

1633

★ The Dutch fort, House of Hope, is built at present-day Hartford.
★ The first permanent European settlement in Connecticut, Windsor, is established by the English.

1634

★ John Oldham and other settlers from Watertown, Massachusetts, found Wethersfield.

1635

★ John Winthrop, Jr., son of Massachusetts governor, establishes Saybrook at the mouth of the Connecticut River.

1636

★ Hartford is started by Thomas Hooker and 100 other Puritans from Newtown (Cambridge, Massachusetts).

1637

★ The Pequot War is fought.

1639

★ Connecticut Colony is formed, and Connecticut's first constitution, the Fundamental Orders, is adopted.

1643

★ Several towns, Branford, Guilford, Milford, Stamford, and Southold (on Long Island) become part of New Haven Colony.

1661

★ John Winthrop, Jr., goes to England to formalize the colony's agreement with England.

1662

★ Connecticut becomes a colony by a royal charter from Charles II.

1664

★ **December:** New Haven Colony agrees to unite with Connecticut Colony.

1675–76

★ Connecticut participates in King Phillip's War, which is waged in Massachusetts and Rhode Island.

1687

★ Sir Edmund Andros assumes control of Connecticut.

1689

★ Andros is arrested after James II is overthrown.

1701

★ The Collegiate School is founded. In 1717 it moves to New Haven, and in 1718 it is renamed Yale College.

1708

★ The Saybrook Platform is adopted to address concerns.

1740

★ Edward and William Pattison in Berlin begin to make tinware.

1745

★ Connecticut troops under Roger Wolcott help capture Louis-bourg on Cape Breton Island during King George's War.

1765

★ Connecticut sends delegates to a meeting of the colonies in New York that demands the British repeal the Stamp Act.

1774

★ Silas Deane, Eliphalet Dyer, and Roger Sherman represent Connecticut at the First Continental Congress in Philadelphia.

1775

★ Several thousand militia go to Massachusetts to help at Lexington, Massachusetts.
★ Troops from Connecticut fight at Fort Ticonderoga.

1776

★ **June 14:** Connecticut passes a resolution for independence.
★ Roger Sherman, a Connecticut judge and legislator, helps write the Declaration of Independence.
★ Samuel Huntington, Roger Sherman, William Williams, and Oliver Wolcott sign the Declaration of Independence.

1777

★ Danbury is attacked by the British.

1779

★ New Haven, Fairfield, and Norwalk are attacked by the British.

1781

★ The British under Benedict Arnold attack New London and Groton.

1787

★ Oliver Ellsworth, William Samuel Johnson, and Roger Sherman represent Connecticut at the Constitutional Convention in Philadelphia. The Constitution is signed by William Samuel Johnson and Roger Sherman.

1788

★ **January 9:** Connecticut ratifies the U.S. Constitution 128 to 40 at a convention in Hartford.

Connecticut
Historical Sites

ANSONIA

General David Humphreys House   Built ca. 1698, the home of Washington's first U.S. ambassador is open to the public.

    Address: 37 Elm Street, Ansonia, CT 06401
    Phone: 203-735-1908
    Web Site: http://derbyhistorical.org/humphrey.htm

BETHLEHEM

Bellamy-Ferriday House and Garden   The Bellamy-Ferriday House was built for Reverend Joseph Bellamy in 1740.

    Address: 9 Main Street North, Bethlehem, CT 06751
    Phone: 203-266-7596
    Web Site: www.hartnet.org/als/alsprop.html

COVENTRY

Nathan Hale Homestead   The Hale family built this house in 1776, the year Nathan Hale was hanged by the British. The house, which is open to the public, is also the site for special Colonial Lifeways programs, Colonial Camp, and other programs.

Address: 2299 South Street, Coventry, CT 06238
Phone: 860-247-8996
Web Site: http://ursamajor.hartnet.org/als/nathanhale

Strong-Porter House Museum   Aaron Strong, Nathan Hale's great uncle, built this farmhouse around 1730. The house, along with a carriage shed, barn, and carpenter's shop are open to the public.

Address: 2382 South Street, Coventry, CT 06238
Phone: 860-742-1419

East Granby

Old Newgate Prison and Copper Mine   Originally a copper mine in the 1700s, Newgate was first used to house serious criminals in 1773. It was the first state prison in America. The prison closed in 1827 and reopened as a mine.

Address: 115 Newgate Road, East Granby, CT 06026
Phone: 860-653-3563
Web Site: www.eastgranby.com/historicalsociety/
  newgateprison2.htm

East Lyme

Thomas Lee House and Little Boston School   Built by Thomas Lee around 1660, the Thomas Lee House is Connecticut's oldest wood-frame house. The Little Boston School, which was built around 1734, was the first school located between Boston and New York City.

Address: Route 156, East Lyme, CT 06357
Phone: 860-739-6070

Farmington

Stanley-Whitman House   John Stanley built the Stanley-Whitman House in 1720. Numerous educational programs are given at the house, and at special events people get the opportunity to spin, weave, make candles, and cook.

Address: 37 High Street, Farmington, CT 06032

Phone: 860-677-9222

Web Site: www.stanleywhitman.org

GREENWICH

Putnam Cottage   Built ca. 1692, during the Revolution, Putnam Cottage was called Knapp's Tavern and was where General Israel Putnam met with other American leaders.

Address: 243 East Putnam Avenue, Greenwich, CT 06830

Phone: 203-869-9697

Web Site: www.putnamcottage.org

GROTON

Fort Griswold Battlefield State Park   On September 6, 1781, Benedict Arnold commanded the 800 British forces who killed 88 of the 165 Patriots who held the fort.

Address: 57 Fort Street, Groton, CT 06340

Phone: 860-449-6877

Web Site: www.revwar.com/ftgriswold

HARTFORD

Ancient Burying Ground of Hartford   Seventeenth-century settlers, including African Americans were buried here, as were soldiers of the Revolution.

Address: corner of Gold and Main Street, Hartford, CT 06103

Phone: 860-561-2585

Butler-McCook House and Garden   Home to generations of Butlers and McCooks, the Butler-McCook House is the oldest house in Hartford.

Address: 396 Main Street, Hartford, CT 06103

Phone: 860-522-1806

Web Site: www.hartnet.org/als/alsprop.html

LEBANON

Governor Jonathan Trumbull House Museum   Jonathan Trumbull, who was governor from 1769 to 1784, lived in this house, which was built by his father between 1735 and 1740.

>   *Address:* West Town Street on the Green, Lebanon, CT 06249
>   *Phone:* 860-642-7558
>   *Web Site:* http://jtrumbulljr.org/museums/governor.shtml

War Office   The Trumbull family store was built ca. 1730. Once the war began, Governor Trumbull had more than 500 meetings of the Council of Safety in the space.

>   *Address:* 149 W. Town Street, Lebanon, CT 06249
>   *Phone:* 860-873-3399
>   *Web Site:* http://jtrumbulljr.org/museums/waroffice.shtml

MERIDEN

Solomon Goffe House   The Solomon Goffe House was built ca. 1711. It is now a living history museum.

>   *Address:* 677 North Colony Street, Meriden, CT 06451
>   *Phone:* 203-634-9088
>   *Web Site:* www.meriden.com/stjoseph/goffe.htm

NEW LONDON

Hempsted Houses   Built in 1678 and inhabited by Joshua Hempsted, a diarist and shipbuilder, the Joshua Hempsted House was home to nine generations of Hempsteds. A rare stone house built in 1759 by Joshua's grandson, Nathaniel Hempsted, is next door.

>   *Address:* 11 Hempsted Street, New London, CT 06320
>   *Phone:* 860-247-8996
>   *Web Site:* www.hartnet.org/als/alsprop.html

Shaw-Perkins Mansion   Built by Captain Nathaniel Shaw in the 1750s, the Shaw-Perkins Mansion was used during the Revolution as Connecticut's naval office. Guided tours that highlight early New London history as well as the trade with the West Indies are available.

Address: 11 Blinman Street, New London, CT 06320

Phone: 860-443-1209

Web Site: www.newlondonhistory.org/mansion1.html

NORWICH

Indian Burial Grounds   The Mohegan chief Uncas, who sided with the colonists against other Indian tribes during the Indian Wars (1637–78), is buried in the Mohegan tribe's burial grounds.

Address: Sachem Street, Norwich, CT 06360

WATERFORD

Colonial Village   A replica of a colonial village, it has the 1740 Jordan Schoolhouse, a blacksmith shop, the 1840 Beebe-Phillips farmhouse, and a barn.

Address: Waterford Historical Society, Jordan Green,
    Route 156, Waterford, CT 06385

Phone: 860-442-2707

WEST HARTFORD

Noah Webster House   Noah Webster, the author of the first American dictionary, was born and raised in this house, which is now open to the public. It depicts life in the mid-18th century.

Address: 227 S. Main Street, West Hartford, CT 06107

Phone: 860-521-5362

Web Site: www.noahwebsterhouse.org

WETHERSFIELD

Buttolph-Williams House   The Buttolph-Williams House was built ca. 1710–20 and is an example of an 18th-century building showing medieval English influence with casement windows and a hewn overhang.

Address: 249 Broad Street, Wethersfield, CT 06109

Phone: 860-247-8996

Web Site: www.hartnet.org/als/alsprop.html

Webb Deane Stevens Museum   Visitors to this museum can tour the colonial houses of Joseph Webb, Silas Deane, and Isaac Stevens—men with strong Revolutionary War connections.

Address: 211 Main Street, Wethersfield, CT 06109
Phone: 860-529-0612
Web Site: www.webb-deane-stevens.org

Further Reading

BOOKS

Fradin, Dennis Brindell. *The Connecticut Colony*. Chicago: Children's Press, 1990.

Girod, Christina M. *Connecticut*. San Diego, Calif.: Lucent, 2002.

Italia, Bob. *The Connecticut Colony*. Edina, Minn.: ABDO, 2001.

Taylor, Robert J. *Colonial Connecticut*. Millwood, N.Y.: KTO Press, 1979.

Whitehurst, Susan. *The Colony of Connecticut*. New York: PowerKids Press, 2000.

WEB SITES

Connecticut History Online. Available online. URL: www.cthistoryonline.org. Downloaded on September 6, 2004.

Noah Webster House. "Connecticut Life in the 1770s." Available online. URL: noahwebsterhouse.org/lifein1770.html. Updated on August 28, 2003.

State of Connecticut. "About Connecticut: Early History." Available online. URL: www.ct.gov/ctportal/cwp/view.asp?a=843&q= 246434. Downloaded on September 6, 2004.

State of Connecticut. "Connect Kids: Connecticut History." Available online. URL: www.kids.state.ct.us/history.htm. Downloaded on September 6, 2004.

Index

Page numbers in *italic* indicate photographs. Page numbers in **boldface** indicate box features. Page numbers followed by m indicate maps. Page numbers followed by c indicate time line entries. Page numbers followed by t indicate tables or graphs.

debt (individual) 94
debt (war)
    from American Revolutionary
       War 94, 96
    French and Indian War 68
    Sugar Act 71
Declaration of Independence 86,
    107c
    first paragraph of the **87**
    Roger Sherman 87, **99**, 107c
Declaratory Act 74
deer 6–7, 7
deerskins 53
Delaware xviiim, 40
depression (economic) 94, 98
direct tax 75
disease
    and Battle of Louisbourg 65
    and Native Americans 13, 15,
       25, 26, **26**
    smallpox 13, 15, 25, 26, **26**
Dominion of New England 40,
    42–45
    Edmund Andros 40
    James II 40, **41**, 41, 43
    map of, 1686-1689 43m
"don't fire until you see the whites of
    their eyes" **84**
drummers 61
dugouts **20**
the Dutch
    Adriaen Block 2, 2, 3, 3m, 4,
       105c
    colonization by xv, xvi, 14, 15
    House of Hope 17, 17, 19, 21,
       105c
    Henry Hudson 1, 1, 2, 15
    William Kieft 30
    land claims by 1, 2, 4, 16–17,
       21, 22
    New Amsterdam 14m, 15, 24
    New Netherland 2, **12**, 14m, 17,
       22, 30, 40
    Pequot Indians 13, 18, 25
    settlement xv, xvi
    tea smuggling 77
    trading of 4, 15–17, 17, 37
Dutch East India Company 1
duties 75
Dyer, Eliphalet 78, 107c

E

earthen mounds xvii
Eastern Woodland Culture 5
education 46–50
    Harvard College 48, 49, **95**
    Native American 10
    The New England Primer **48**
    one-room schoolhouses **46,** 49
    Yale University 49, 50, 50, 106c
effigy, hanging in 73
Ellsworth, Oliver 98, 100, 108c
Endecott, John 27, 28
England. *See also* British forces; Parlia-
    ment
    John Cabot 1
    Charles I 36–37, **39, 41**
    Charles II 38–40, **39**, 39, **41,**
       106c
    Church of England **16**, 36, 45
    civil war in 36–38, 37, **39**
    colonial wars of 60, 62–66,
       68–70
    colonists allegiance to 75
    colonization by xvi, 4, 14,
       19–22
    control of colonies by 38–40
    Oliver Cromwell 36–37, 37, **39,**
       41
    French and Indian War 60, 66,
       67, **67, 68,** 68–70, **82**
    Henry VIII **16**
    James II 40, 41, **41**, 43, 45,
       106c
    land claims of 1, 68
    Battle of Louisbourg 65
    Protestants in **41**
    restoration of the monarchy in
       38–40
    settlement by xvi, 4, 19–22, 25
    Spain xv
    surrender at Yorktown 93
    William and Mary 44
    Windsor, Connecticut 105c
equal representation **99,** 100
Europe. *See also specific headings, e.g.:* Eng-
    land
    15th-century xiii, xiv
    Dark Ages xiii
    land claims by 1, 2
    view of Native Americans xvii

Europeans
    influences on Native Americans
       by 11–13
    world view of 7
exploration
    Africa xv
    Adriaen Block 2, 2, 3, 3m, 4,
       105c
    John Cabot 1
    Christopher Columbus xiii, xv,
       52
    Henry Hudson 1, 1, 2, 15
    Giovanni da Verrazano 1
    Vikings xiii, xiv

F

Fairfield, Connecticut 92, 107c
Far East xiii–xv
farmers
    in Connecticut 94, 96
    debt of 94
    rebellion of 94
farming 46. *See also* crops; plantations
    along Connecticut River 18
    life on the farm 50, 53–55
    by Native Americans 5, 6, 10
    slavery **55**
    support of war effort by 88
    tobacco 53
federal government, taxation by 96,
    98
Federalists 98
Fenwick, George 20
First Continental Congress. *See* Conti-
    nental Congress, First
fishing 6, 10
Fitch, Thomas 73
flax 50
fleet (English) 62, 65
Fletcher, Benjamin 60, 61
Florida xv, 68
food (as currency) **12**
Fort Griswold. *See* Griswold, Fort
Fort Ticonderoga. *See* Ticonderoga, Fort
France
    Albany Plan **69**
    and alliances with Native Ameri-
       cans 60, **67**
    assistance in American Revolu-
       tion 93

Intolerable Acts 77
  reaction to Boston Tea Party 77
  Stamp Act of 1765 72, 74, **74**
  Sugar Act 71
  Tea Act 76
  Townshend Duties 76
Patriots **89**
  Boston Port Bills 77
  Breed's Hill 83
  in Massachusetts 80
  Sons of Liberty 72, 73, 74, **74,**
    76, 77, 78, **82**
  Townshend Duties 75
Pattison, Edward 56, 107c
Pattison, William 56, 107c
Paugusset Indians 5m
Pennsylvania xviiim
Pepperell, William 62, 64, 65
Pequot Indians 4, 5m
  destruction of 13
  and the Dutch 13, 18, 25
  and English expansion 27
  housing of 9, 10
  Mohegan Indians 13
  and neighboring tribes 11
  John Oldham 27
  Sassacus 25, 27, 29, 30
  trade 13, 25
  villages of the 11, 28, 29
Pequot War 25, 27–30, 106c
  attack on Narragansetts 28
  and attack on village near Mystic
    28, 29
  John Mason 27, 28, 29
Philip, King. See Metacom
Pierson, Abraham 49
pigs 54
Pilgrims **16**
  Mayflower 15
  settlement by 18
pipes **52**
plantations. See also crops; farming
  slavery 13
  tobacco **52**
playing cards 72
Plymouth Colony 15–17
  display of Metacom's head at 34
  land claims of 22, 23
  Pilgrims **16**
  Puritans from the 4

religious tolerance 18
  and Rhode Island 33
Plymouth Virginia Company 15
Pocumtuc Indians 33
podunk, derivation of the term 4
Podunk Indians 4, 5m
popcorn **6**
Pope, Hannah **82**
population
  in 1640 24, 46, 51t
  in 1670 31
  in 1760 46, 51t
  African Americans in, 1760 **55**
  growth of 46, 51t
  killed in King Phillip's War 35
  of Native Americans xvii, 4
  representation based on **99,**
    100
  of towns 58
Port Royal, Nova Scotia 62
Potatuck Indians 4, 5m
Praying Indians 32, 33
Prescott, William 83, **84**
primers 47, **48**
prisoners 62
privateers 89–91
  French and Indian War 66
  in New London/Groton 93
Protestant Reformation xiv
Protestants **16**
  in England **41**
  settlement by xvi
protests
  Boston Tea Party **74,** 76, 77
  James Ingersoll 73, 74
  Stamp Act 73, 74, **74**
  Townshend Duties 75–76
Puritans **16**
  Edmund Andros 40, 40, 42, 42,
    42, 44–45, 106c
  colony of New Haven 22, 23
  Congregationalists **54,** 54–55
  Oliver Cromwell 36–37, 37, **39,**
    41
  defeat of, in England **39**
  and education 46
  Reverend Thomas Hooker 19,
    19, 20, 105c
  Massachusetts Bay Colony 4,
    16

migration of 36–38
  and Native Americans 27
  New Haven 24
  in Parliament 36
  Plymouth Colony 4
  public drunkenness 55
  settlement by 4, 15, 16, 18
  work ethic of 54
Putnam, Israel 74, **82,** 83
  Breed's Hill 82
  French and Indian War 66, **82**
  raid on Greenwich 91
  Sons of Liberty 72
Putnam Cottage 111

Q

Quartering Act 78
Quebec
  Samuel de Champlain 15
  French and Indian War **67, 68**
Quebec Act 78
Queen Anne's War 60, 62
Quinipi Indians 5m
Quinnehtukqut 3, 4
Quinnipiac River 24
Quirpi Indians 4

R

raids (by British forces) 91–93,
  107c, 108c
ratification of U.S. Constitution
  101–103, 108c
rattles 7
redcoats 82. See also British forces
religion. See also specific headings, e.g.:
  Christianity
    Congregationalists 54–55
    Native Americans 6–8
    Saybrook Platform **54**
    Sunday 54
religious freedom 16
religious tolerance 18, 44–45
Renaissance xiv
Rhode Island xviiim, 106c
  Adriaen Block 4
  expansion by 32, 33
  Battle of Louisbourg 64
  Native Americans 32
  slavery **55**
  Sons of Liberty 72